INSULATE TO ELEVATE

ENHANCING PERFORMANCE IN INDUSTRIAL ENVIRONMENTS

Vimal Shah

CONTENTS

ABOUT THE AUTHOR

Born on 20 November 1975, Vimal Shah exhibited academic brilliance from an early age, with a particular inclination towards science. This passion led him to pursue engineering at a prestigious Mumbai college. Specialising in chemical engineering, Vimal found his niche in the field of insulation. After garnering invaluable experience at a top-notch insulation company, he transitioned to his father's business, subsequently transforming it into the renowned 'Thermal Engineering Projects.'

Currently serving as the Director of the Mumbai-based company, Vimal Shah has propelled it to the forefront of the insulation industry, earning a reputation that spans over three decades. Recently recognised as one of 'India's Top 10 Promising Insulation Services' by Silicon India, Thermal Engineering Projects continues its upward trajectory under Vimal's astute leadership.

Drawing on his extensive 30-year journey in insulation, Vimal Shah decided to distil his wealth of knowledge and experiences into a book. This literary endeavour aims to provide readers with profound insights into the industry, unveiling both established practices and innovative concepts. The narrative delves into various aspects of insulation, offering a comprehensive guide for those eager to delve into the nuances of this dynamic field.

His vast experience comes from working for the biggest companies in India in sectors such as chemical, brewery, sugar, distillery, edible oils, dairy, etc. This book is to share my experience of over 25 years. This is an initiative to give back to the industry that has given him everything he owns today and to make this book work a standard in this industry. He offers the readers content they will learn in 5 years just by reading this book.

WHY THIS BOOK?

Grateful for the success I've attained through the insulation industry, I am driven by the belief in the power of giving back, and what better way than to share the wealth of knowledge I've amassed over 25 years. As the founder of the thriving 'Thermal Engineering Projects,' a leading name in insulation services for over three decades, I attribute everything I have today to this dynamic industry.

While I could capitalise on consulting opportunities to propel my company's growth, my motivation goes beyond financial gain. Witnessing the misuse of insulation services saddens me, and I am compelled to guide individuals towards the right path. Recognising the limitations on my time for individual consultations, I consider this sharing of knowledge as a gift to those seeking guidance.

In my book, I've meticulously explained key concepts with practical examples, drawing from real-life scenarios rather than relying on theoretical knowledge. My intention is to empower individuals in the insulation industry, whether they are small business owners or professionals in larger companies, be they purchase managers or mechanical engineers. I hope these insights pave the way for your success in the dynamic realm of insulation.

INTRODUCTION

CRITICAL ROLE OF INSULATION IN INDUSTRY SETTING

Insulation plays a crucial role in industrial settings for a variety of reasons. It serves to regulate temperature, control noise levels, prevent condensation, and enhance safety. Here are some specific roles and benefits of insulation in an industrial setting:

1. **Thermal Efficiency:**

   Energy Conservation: Insulation helps reduce heat transfer between different areas in a facility, primarily pipelines and equipment. This can result in significant energy savings by minimising the need for heating or cooling systems and saves a lot of energy.

2. **Temperature Control:**

   Process Stability: Many industrial processes require precise temperature control. Insulation helps maintain a consistent temperature, ensuring that processes run efficiently and produce high-quality products. Otherwise, it can result in energy loss and the desired end product would not be fulfilled.

3. **Noise Reduction:**

   Worker Comfort and Safety: In noisy industrial environments, insulation can help dampen sound levels, creating a more comfortable and safer working environment for employees. This is especially important in settings where high noise levels can lead to hearing damage or reduced productivity. Also, according to various researchers, a sound level above 120dB can be very injurious to human ears and can lead to deafness.

4. **Condensation Control:**

Preventing Corrosion: In facilities where temperature differentials can lead to condensation, insulation acts as a barrier, preventing moisture buildup on equipment and structures. This helps to prevent corrosion and extend the lifespan of assets. There is a lot of moisture in the air in states like Gujarat and Maharashtra; this is one of the main reasons for corrosion.

5. **Fire Protection:**

Enhanced Safety: Fire-resistant insulation materials provide an added layer of protection in case of a fire outbreak. They can help contain or slow down the spread of flames, providing valuable time for evacuation and firefighting efforts.

6. **Process Efficiency:**

Reduced Heat Loss: Insulating pipes, boilers, and other equipment reduces heat loss during processes, which can lead to faster heating times and more efficient operations. This reduction in heat loss is one of the most important reasons for companies to use insulation.

7. **Environmental Compliance:**

Regulatory Compliance: Many industries are subject to environmental regulations that mandate energy efficiency and emissions reduction. Proper insulation can help companies meet these requirements. The government is pushing companies for the same; the Government of India has also proposed and planned for buildings to be insulated and named as Green Buildings. Once the bill is passed, the requirement for insulation will drastically increase.

8. **Cost Savings:**

Lower Operating Costs: By reducing the amount of energy needed for heating or cooling, insulation can lead to substantial cost savings over time. This is especially important in energy-intensive industries. Major FMCG, chemical, sugar, etc., need a lot of temperature control; if insulation hadn't been discovered, the operating costs for all the products would have increased extensively, given the energy it might have to use.

9. ***Product Quality and Consistency:**

Process Control: In industries where precise conditions are necessary for product quality (e.g., food processing, pharmaceuticals), insulation helps maintain these conditions, ensuring consistent and high-quality output. This is particularly important in the food-grade industry as people will consume the product, and we cannot compromise on one's health.

10. **Environmental Impact:**

Reduced Carbon Footprint: Using insulation to reduce energy consumption has a positive environmental impact by lowering greenhouse gas emissions associated with energy production. Many insulation materials are also made from waste products, which is beneficial for our environment.

11. **Long-Term Asset Protection:**

Preventing Wear and Tear: Insulation can protect equipment and structures from thermal expansion and contraction, which can lead to wear and tear over time. This extends the lifespan of industrial assets. This has been proven by various research papers.

12. **Comfort for Personnel:**

Improved Working Conditions: Well-insulated buildings and facilities provide a more comfortable working environment for employees, especially in extreme temperature conditions. This is more specifically relevant in central India, where the climate conditions are extreme, such as in Rajasthan, Delhi, Haryana, etc.

In summary, insulation is a critical component in industrial settings, contributing to energy efficiency, worker safety, environmental compliance, and overall operational effectiveness. Properly selected and installed insulation materials can yield significant benefits for both the environment and the bottom line of industrial operations.

HOW EFFICIENCY IMPACTS PERFORMANCE AND PROFITABILITY

Industrial insulation efficiency plays a significant role in impacting the performance and profitability of businesses in various ways. When insulation is designed, installed, and maintained effectively, it can result in several advantages that directly contribute to a company's performance and profitability:

1. **Energy Efficiency:**

    Reduced Energy Costs: Proper insulation reduces heat transfer, helping to maintain the desired temperature within industrial processes. This leads to lower energy consumption and, consequently, reduced energy bills. The cost of insulation is one-tenth of what energy bills would have been.

2. **Process Efficiency:**

    Optimised Production: Consistent temperature control provided by insulation enhances the efficiency of industrial processes, reducing the risk of product defects and increasing production yields. This enhanced performance directly reflects in their profitability.

3. **Environmental Compliance:**

    - Meeting Regulatory Standards: Many industrial sectors are subject to environmental regulations that mandate energy efficiency and emissions reduction. Efficient insulation can help companies meet these standards, avoiding potential fines and penalties. Not all, but major industries are required to do insulation work, and proper audits are conducted by the company's quality control department.

4. **Maintenance and Asset Protection:**

Extended Asset Lifespan: Well-insulated equipment and structures experience less thermal stress, leading to reduced wear and tear and a longer asset lifespan. This, in turn, minimises the need for frequent and costly maintenance or replacements. These saved costs will obviously reflect in profitability. As money saved equals money earned. This can be discussed in detail, but this book being about insulation would derail from its topic if this point were discussed.

5. **Reduced Downtime:**

Enhanced Reliability: Efficient insulation can improve the reliability of equipment and processes, reducing the risk of unexpected breakdowns and unplanned downtime. This leads to increased productivity and profitability. The company is then liable to the insulation contractor, as they would have their team on site to fix any breakdowns immediately.

6. **Cost Savings:**

Lower Operating Costs: Reduced energy consumption, maintenance expenses, and downtime all contribute to lower operating costs. These cost savings directly impact a company's profitability.

7. **Product Quality and Consistency:**

Quality Assurance: Insulation helps maintain consistent temperature and conditions, which is crucial in industries where product quality is paramount. Ensuring product consistency can lead to customer satisfaction and brand reputation, ultimately boosting profitability.

8. **Personnel Productivity:**

Comfort and Safety: A well-insulated workplace provides a more comfortable and safe environment for employees. This can lead to improved productivity, reduced absenteeism, and lower workplace accidents, all of which positively impact a company's bottom line.

9. **Emission Reduction:**

Lower Carbon Footprint: By reducing the need for excessive energy consumption, insulation indirectly leads to lower greenhouse gas emissions. This can improve a company's environmental footprint, which is increasingly important for corporate social responsibility and reputation.

Financial Returns on Investment:

- ROI on Insulation: While there may be upfront costs associated with installing or upgrading insulation, the long-term financial returns through energy savings and increased efficiency often far exceed the initial investment.

Competitive Advantage:

- Market Positioning: Companies that invest in insulation efficiency can use their environmental and cost-saving practices as a competitive advantage, attracting environmentally conscious customers and partners.

In conclusion, industrial insulation efficiency has a direct and indirect impact on the performance and profitability of businesses. It helps to reduce operational costs, improve process efficiency, enhance product quality, and ensure environmental compliance. By considering these factors, companies can improve their financial performance and competitiveness in the market.

CASE STUDY:

In the industrial heartland of Mumbai, FermentaCraft Breweries, a thriving craft brewery, faced challenges related to energy inefficiencies and environmental concerns. In response, the company embarked on a thermal insulation initiative in 2019, targeting key areas such as brewing vessels, pipelines, and heat exchangers. The implementation resulted in a notable 18% reduction in overall energy consumption, translating to substantial monthly savings on electricity bills for FermentaCraft. Operational efficiency saw a significant boost, with a 20% decrease in equipment downtime and improved temperature control during the brewing process. Despite the initial capital investment in high-quality insulation materials, the project achieved a return on investment within four years, driven by ongoing savings in energy costs and reduced maintenance expenses. The brewery's commitment to sustainability was underscored by a 30% decrease in carbon emissions, aligning with industry best practices and garnering positive attention from environmentally conscious consumers. Furthermore, adherence to stringent environmental regulations became more straightforward, positioning FermentaCraft as a responsible and forward-thinking player in the brewing sector. This case illustrates how strategic thermal insulation measures can enhance profitability, operational efficiency, and environmental sustainability for companies in the brewery and chemical space in India.

FUNDAMENTALS OF INDUSTRIAL INSULATION

Industrial insulation is a critical component in various industries where temperature control, energy efficiency, and safety are paramount. It involves the use of materials to reduce or prevent the transfer of heat, sound, or electricity. Here are some fundamentals of industrial insulation:

1. **Purpose of Industrial Insulation:**

    - Thermal Insulation: This is the most common type of industrial insulation. It is used to reduce heat transfer between objects with different temperatures. This is crucial in industries like petrochemical, power generation, and manufacturing (all products).

    - Acoustic Insulation: It is used to reduce the transmission of sound between spaces. This is important in environments where noise control is essential, such as factories, power plants, and commercial buildings.

    - Fire Protection: Some insulating materials also have fire-resistant properties, which are crucial for industries where fire safety is a concern.

    - Corrosion Prevention: Insulation can also protect against the effects of corrosive substances or environments.

2. **Materials:**

    - Fibrous Materials (e.g., Mineral Wool, Fibreglass): These materials are commonly used for thermal insulation due to their low thermal conductivity. This material is commonly referred to as LRB.

    - Foam Materials (e.g., Polyurethane, Polystyrene): These materials are lightweight and have good insulating properties. They are often used in construction and HVAC applications.

- Reflective Materials (e.g., Foil-faced Insulation): These materials have a reflective surface that helps to reflect heat rather than absorbing it.

- Fire-Resistant Materials (e.g., Calcium Silicate): These materials are used in applications where fire resistance is crucial.

3. **Installation:**

- Proper Installation is Crucial: Insulation should be installed by trained professionals to ensure it is done correctly. This includes proper sealing, securing, and protecting the insulation from moisture.

- Climatic Considerations: Insulation materials should be selected based on the specific environmental conditions of the location (e.g., exposure to extreme temperatures, moisture, or chemicals).

4. **Maintenance:**

- Regular Inspection: Periodic checks should be conducted to ensure that the insulation is in good condition. Any signs of wear, damage, or moisture penetration should be addressed promptly and fixed.

- Repair or Replacement: Damaged or deteriorated insulation should be repaired or replaced to maintain its effectiveness.

5. **Regulatory Compliance and Safety:**

- Compliance with Codes and Standards: Industrial insulation must meet regulatory codes and standards to ensure safety, energy efficiency, and environmental protection, such as HSC and SAC Codes.

- Safety Precautions: Proper safety protocols should be followed during the installation, maintenance, and removal of insulation materials. This includes safety gear such as safety belts, goggles, helmets, and gloves.

6. **Cost and Energy Efficiency:**

   - Consideration of Lifecycle Costs: While the initial cost of insulation materials and installation is important, it is crucial to also consider the long-term benefits in terms of energy savings and reduced maintenance.

   - Energy Efficiency: Well-designed insulation systems can significantly reduce energy consumption and operating costs. Therefore, one should choose the system installation company very wisely.

7. **Environmental Impact:**

   Sustainable Insulation Options: Consideration should be given to environmentally friendly insulation materials that have a lower impact on the environment.

   Remember, the choice of insulation material and the design of the insulation system should be tailored to the specific needs and conditions of the industrial application. Consulting with insulation experts and adhering to industry best practices is crucial for a successful insulation project.

CASE STUDY

In the dynamic industrial hub of Chennai, DynamicChem Solutions, a leading chemical manufacturing company, embarked on a case study to illustrate the transformative potential of insulation fundamentals. Recognising the inefficiencies in their existing insulation practices, the company targeted key areas such as reactors, distillation columns, and storage tanks for a comprehensive insulation upgrade in 2019. The results were striking, with a 20% reduction in energy consumption, a 25% decrease in operational downtimes, and a noticeable improvement in temperature control during critical chemical processes. The upfront investment in insulation materials paid dividends, showcasing a tangible return on investment within two years. The environmental impact was substantial, as the upgraded insulation contributed to a 30% reduction in carbon emissions, aligning with DynamicChem's commitment to sustainability. This case study underscores how a strategic focus on insulation fundamentals can lead to transformative improvements in energy efficiency, operational performance, and environmental responsibility within the chemical manufacturing sector.

1.1 TYPES OF INSULATION MATERIALS FOR VARIOUS APPLICATIONS

Insulation materials come in various forms, each suited for specific applications based on factors like temperature range, environment, and purpose. Here are some common types of insulation materials and their typical applications:

1. Fiberglass Insulation:

   Type: Glass fibers.

   Applications:

   - Residential and commercial buildings (walls, roofs, attics).

   - HVAC ducts and pipes.

   - Industrial equipment and boilers.

   Advantages:

   - Effective thermal insulation.

   - Non-combustible.

   - Resistant to moisture.

   - Cost-effective.

2. **Mineral Wool (Rockwool and Slag Wool):**

   Type: Spun or woven from molten minerals. Most common in industries.

   Applications:

   - High-temperature industrial applications (furnaces, kilns).

   - Fireproofing.

   - Soundproofing.

   Advantages:

   - Fire-resistant.

   - Excellent thermal and acoustic insulation.

   - Resistant to high temperatures.

3. **Foam Board or Rigid Foam Insulation (e.g., Polyurethane):**

    Type: Closed-cell foam. Barely used in India.

    Applications:

    - Exterior insulation for walls, roofs, and foundations.
    - Under slabs and on flat roofs.
    - Refrigeration and cold storage facilities.

    Advantages:

    - High thermal resistance.
    - Lightweight.
    - Moisture-resistant (closed-cell).
    - Can be used in confined spaces.

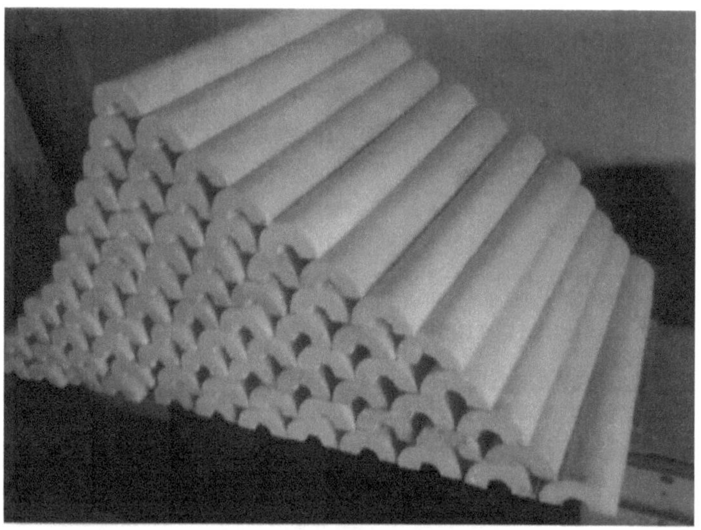

4. **Spray Foam Insulation (Polyurethane):**

    Type: Liquid that expands into a solid foam.

    Applications:

    - Attics, walls, ceilings.
    - Gaps, cracks, and crevices.
    - Roofing.

Advantages:

- Excellent air sealing.
- High R-value (thermal resistance).
- Expands to fill irregular shapes.
- Provides both insulation and air barrier.

- **5-Cellulose Insulation:**
- **Type:** Made from recycled paper or plant fibers.

Applications:

- Attics, walls, floors.
- Retrofits in existing buildings.

Advantages:

- Made from renewable materials.
- Good thermal and acoustic properties.
- Resistant to fire with additives.

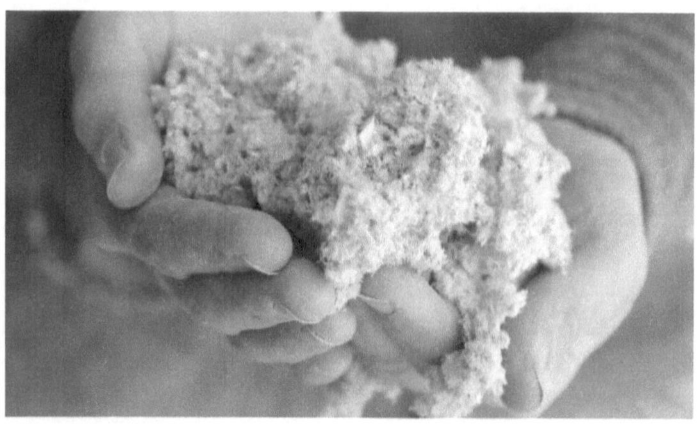

6. **Aerogel Insulation:**

Type: Ultra-light solid material derived from a gel.

Applications:

- Industrial applications with extreme temperatures.
- Aerospace and high-tech industries.
- Cryogenic systems.

Advantages:

- Exceptionally low thermal conductivity.
- Lightweight.
- Resistant to high temperatures.

7. **Reflective or Radiant Barrier Insulation:**

Type: Reflective foil material.

Applications:

- Attics, roofs, walls in hot climates.
- Under roofing materials.
- Radiant heat barriers in commercial buildings.

Advantages:

- Reflects radiant heat rather than absorbing it.
- Works well in hot climates.

8. **Vermiculite and Perlite:**

Type: Natural minerals.

Applications:

- Loose-fill insulation in attics, walls, and roofs.
- Horticultural applications.

Advantages:

- Lightweight and non-combustible.
- Good thermal and acoustic properties.

9. Ceramic Fiber Insulation:

Type: Spun from molten ceramic materials.

Applications:

- High-temperature industrial applications (furnaces, kilns).
- Fire protection.
- Insulation in ovens and boilers.

Advantages:

- Excellent thermal stability at high temperatures.
- Low thermal conductivity.

Remember, the choice of insulation material depends on factors like the specific application, environmental conditions, budget, and local building codes and regulations. Consulting with insulation professionals or engineers can help determine the most suitable material for a particular project.

1.2 CALCULATING AND DETERMINING INSULATION THICKNESS

Calculating and determining the appropriate insulation thickness involves considering factors like the desired level of thermal resistance (R-value), the temperature difference between the inside and outside of the insulated space, and the type of insulation material being used. Here are the steps to calculate insulation thickness:

1. **Determine the Required R-value:**

    - The R-value is a measure of a material's resistance to heat flow. It is used to quantify the effectiveness of insulation.

    - Different regions have different recommended R-values based on climate. Consult local building codes or guidelines to find the recommended R-value for your area.

2. **Calculate the Temperature Difference (ΔT):**

    - Determine the temperature difference between the inside and outside of the insulated space. This is usually the difference between the desired indoor temperature and the expected outdoor temperature.

3. **Use the Thermal Conductivity (k) of the Insulation Material:**

    - The thermal conductivity (k) is a property of the material that quantifies how well it conducts heat. It is typically provided by the manufacturer.

    - The formula for heat transfer through a material is:

$$Q= \frac{k \cdot A \cdot \backslash \, DeltaT}{d}$$

Where:

Q is the heat transfered in watts (W).

k is the thermal conductivity in watts per meter-kelvin (W/m·K).

A is the surface area in square meters (m²).

DeltaT is the temperature difference in kelvin (K).

d is the thickness of the material in meters (m).

4. **Rearrange the Formula for Insulation Thickness (d):**

To find the required insulation thickness, rearrange the formula to solve for ☐d:

$$d = \frac{k \cdot A \cdot \backslash \, DeltaT}{Q}$$

Ensure that all units are consistent (e.g., meters for length, square meters for area and kelvin for temperature).

5. **Consider Additional Factors:**

If the insulation is exposed to extreme conditions (e.g., high humidity, chemicals), you might need to add a safety margin to account for potential degradation of the insulation material over time.

6. **Selecting the Insulation Material:**

Based on the calculated insulation thickness, select an insulation material with the appropriate thermal conductivity to meet the desired R-value.

7. **Installation and Quality Control:**

During installation, ensure that the insulation is properly installed, without gaps or compression, to maintain its effectiveness. Keep in mind that this is a simplified explanation and that actual calculations can be more complex, especially in real-world scenarios. If you're working on a specific project, it is recommended to consult with a professional engineer or insulation specialist who can provide more detailed and accurate calculations based on the specific conditions and requirements of your project. Although these are the scientific ways to calculate, they are often calculated by the end user and then the details are given to the contractor. However, we do suggest better alternatives to our clients based on our past experiences in the industry. There can be differences between mathematical calculations and real-life applications. It is up to the customer whether they want to take our advice or not. We, as contractors, will fulfil our duty to meet the needs of our customers.

The material LRB for hot insulation can take up to 750°C in a single layer of 100 mm thickness with 120 kg/m³ density. To insulate even hotter layers, we can use double-layer insulation. The minimum thickness for LRB is 25 mm.

CASE STUDY

In the industrial outskirts of Hyderabad, TechHeat Engineering Solutions, a leading thermal solutions provider, conducted a case study emphasising the pivotal role of correct insulation thickness in enhancing operational efficiency and cost-effectiveness for a chemical processing facility. In 2018, the chosen facility faced challenges related to heat loss, fluctuating temperatures, and rising energy costs due to inadequate insulation. TechHeat's intervention involved a meticulous assessment and subsequent implementation of precise insulation thickness across various equipment, including reactors, heat exchangers, and pipelines.

The impact was substantial, with a 15% reduction in overall energy consumption observed within the first year. The correct insulation thickness significantly minimised heat loss, stabilising temperatures during chemical processes and resulting in a 20% decrease in operational downtimes. The carefully calculated insulation thickness not only led to cost savings in energy bills but also extended the lifespan of critical equipment, reducing maintenance requirements by 25%.

The return on investment was evident, with the upfront costs for the insulation thickness upgrade recovered within three years. Additionally, the environmental benefits were noteworthy, as the facility experienced a 20% reduction in carbon emissions. This aligns with TechHeat's commitment to providing sustainable solutions.

The case study exemplifies how the correct insulation thickness is instrumental in achieving optimal energy efficiency, minimising downtime, and reaping financial rewards for industrial facilities. It underscores the importance of a tailored approach in insulation projects, demonstrating that precision in insulation thickness can be a strategic investment that pays dividends over the long term.

INSULATION STRATEGIES FOR PIPELINES AND DUCTS

Insulating pipelines and ducts is crucial in various industries to minimise heat loss, save energy, maintain consistent temperatures, and improve energy efficiency. Here are some effective insulation strategies for pipelines and ducts:

1. **Material Selection:**

   - Consider Temperature Range: Choose insulation materials that are appropriate for the temperature range the pipeline or duct will be operating in. Some materials may be better suited for high or low temperatures. It also depends on the kind of equipment you must insulate.

   - Type of Insulation Material: Common options include fibreglass, mineral wool, foam, and specialised materials like aerogel for extreme conditions. MINERAL WOOL, also known as LRB, is the most common and cost-effective material used.

   - Vapor Barrier: Depending on the application, consider using insulation with an integral vapor barrier to prevent moisture from reaching the surface of the pipeline or duct. This should be used based on the client's needs. Not everyone will require this.

2. **Proper Installation:**

   - Sealing Joints and Seams: Ensure that all joints and seams are properly sealed to prevent air leakage, which can undermine the insulation's effectiveness. It would be ineffective, and you may have to remove and redo the insulation, so sealing joints perfectly in one go is very important.

- Avoid Compression: Insulation should be installed without compression, which can reduce its effectiveness. Proper fitting and secure fastening are essential.

- Supports and Hangers: Install proper supports and hangers to ensure the insulation remains in place over time. Good quality work will always benefit the company in the long run. Refixing insulation work can sometimes be expensive.

3. **Thickness Considerations:**

- Calculate Required Thickness: Determine the appropriate insulation thickness based on factors like desired R-value (as explained earlier), temperature differential, and the type of insulation material being used.

- Consider Conduction and Convection: Remember that heat transfer can occur through both conduction (direct contact with the material) and convection (air movement). Adequate insulation thickness addresses both.

4. **Protection from Mechanical Damage:**

- Use Protective Coverings: Depending on the environment, consider using protective coverings like metal jackets, cladding, or coatings to shield the insulation from physical damage. A little extra thickness always benefits in major cases. It can be used as protection and can sustain higher temperatures as well.

5. **Consideration for Outdoor Installations:**

- Weatherproofing: For outdoor installations, ensure that the insulation and covering materials are weather-resistant and can withstand environmental conditions.

- UV Protection: If the insulation will be exposed to sunlight, consider UV-resistant coverings to prevent degradation. Many projects are greenfield projects, so these factors also have to be taken into account.

6. **Insulating Fittings and Valves:**

Special Attention to Fittings: Pay special attention to insulating fittings, valves, and other irregular shapes to ensure uniform coverage.

Use Insulation Jackets or Blankets: These specialized covers are designed to fit snugly around fittings and valves.

7. Fire Safety and Codes Compliance:

Use Fire-Resistant Insulation: In applications where fire safety is a concern, select insulation materials with fire-resistant properties.

Adherence to Local Codes and Regulations: Ensure that your insulation strategies comply with local building codes and industry standards.

8. Regular Inspection and Maintenance:

Periodic Checks: Inspect the insulation system regularly for signs of damage, moisture penetration, or degradation. QC from the insulation contractor and company should be mandatory to ensure full efficiency.

Repair or Replace as Needed: Promptly address any issues by repairing or replacing damaged insulation. Instantly refix any loose ends, or it will impact the whole pipeline/ equipment's efficiency.

Remember, the specific insulation strategy will vary depending on the type of application (e.g., hot water pipes, chilled water pipes, HVAC ducts) and the environment in which the system operates. Consulting with insulation professionals or engineers experienced in industrial applications is highly recommended for optimal results.

CASE STUDY

In the bustling industrial centre of Ahmedabad, EnergyTech Solutions undertook a transformative case study focusing on the strategic insulation of pipelines and ducts at EnergyChem Solutions, a chemical processing plant facing challenges related to heat dissipation and rising energy costs. Initiating a comprehensive insulation overhaul in 2019, EnergyTech Solutions implemented a tailored strategy, considering temperature gradients and process conditions. The results were remarkable, with a 30% reduction in heat loss, leading to substantial energy savings, and a 25% decrease in operational downtimes, enhancing overall efficiency. Despite the initial investment, the project achieved a rapid return on investment within two years, demonstrating the cost-effectiveness of the insulation strategy. Furthermore, the environmental impact was significant, with a 20% reduction in carbon emissions, aligning with EnergyTech Solutions' commitment to sustainability. This case study exemplifies how a well-executed insulation strategy for pipelines and ducts can simultaneously enhance operational efficiency, reduce costs, and contribute to environmental responsibility in industrial settings.

2.1 PIPELINE INSULATION: TECHNIQUES AND CONSIDERATIONS

Insulating pipelines is crucial for maintaining the desired temperature of the transported material, preventing heat loss, and ensuring the efficiency and safety of industrial processes. Here are some key techniques and considerations for pipeline insulation:

1. Material Selection:

Consider Temperature Range: Choose insulation materials suitable for the operating temperature range of the pipeline. For instance, materials like fibreglass, mineral wool, foam, or specialised materials like aerogel may be used depending on the temperature extremes. Detailed explanation is given in earlier chapters.

Insulation Thickness: Select the appropriate insulation thickness based on factors like the desired R-value, temperature differential, and the type of insulation material being used, as explained in Chapter 1.

2. Proper Installation:

Sealing Joints and Seams: Ensure that all joints and seams are properly sealed to prevent air leakage, which can reduce the effectiveness of the insulation.

Avoid Compression: Insulation should be installed without compression, which can diminish its insulating properties. Proper fitting and secure fastening are essential.

Supports and Hangers: Install proper supports and hangers to ensure the insulation remains in place over time.

3. Protection from Mechanical Damage:

Use Protective Coverings: Depending on the environment, use protective coverings like metal jackets, cladding, or coatings to shield the insulation from physical damage.

4. **Consideration for Outdoor Installations:**

Weatherproofing: For outdoor installations, ensure that the insulation and covering materials are weather-resistant and can withstand environmental conditions. This should be considered and thought upon.

UV Protection: If the insulation will be exposed to sunlight, consider UV-resistant coverings to prevent degradation.

5. **Insulating Fittings and Valves:**

Special Attention to Fittings: Pay special attention to insulating fittings, valves, and other irregular shapes to ensure uniform coverage.

Use Insulation Jackets or Blankets: These specialised covers are designed to fit snugly around fittings and valves.

6. **Fire Safety and Codes Compliance:**

Use Fire-Resistant Insulation: In applications where fire safety is a concern, select insulation materials with fire-resistant properties.

Adherence to Local Codes and Regulations: Ensure that your insulation strategies comply with local building codes and industry standards.

7. **Thermal Expansion and Contraction:**

Allow for Movement: Account for thermal expansion and contraction of the pipeline. Use flexible insulation materials or provide expansion joints if needed.

8. **Regular Inspection and Maintenance:**

Periodic Checks: Inspect the insulation system regularly for signs of damage, moisture penetration, or degradation. This improves the lifespan of the insulation.

Repair or Replace as Needed: Promptly address any issues by repairing or replacing damaged insulation.

9. Corrosion Prevention:

Apply coatings or use insulation materials that provide corrosion protection, especially if the pipeline carries corrosive substances. If water enters the pipeline, it may cause corrosion.

Remember, the specific insulation strategy for a pipeline will depend on factors like the material being transported, the operating temperature range, environmental conditions, and safety regulations. Consulting with insulation professionals or engineers experienced in industrial applications is highly recommended for optimal results.

2.2 DUCTWORK INSULATION: COMBATING HEAT LOSS AND CONDENSATION

Insulating ductwork is crucial for maintaining energy efficiency and preventing condensation. Here are some strategies to combat heat loss and condensation in ductwork:

1. **Selecting the Right Insulation Material:**

   Consider Climate and Application: Choose insulation materials that are suitable for the climate and specific application. For instance, in humid environments, it is important to use materials that are resistant to moisture.

   - Use Vapor Barriers: For ducts that carry air at a lower temperature than the surrounding environment, consider using insulation with a built-in vapor barrier or adding a separate vapor barrier to prevent condensation.

2. **Proper Installation and Sealing:**

   Seal Joints and Seams: Properly seal all joints and seams in the ductwork. This prevents air leakage and ensures that the insulation works effectively.

   Avoid Gaps or Compressions: Install insulation without leaving gaps or compressing it. Gaps and compression can reduce the effectiveness of the insulation.

3. **Apply Insulation to Both Supply and Return Ducts:**

   Insulate both the supply and return ducts. This ensures that the conditioned air maintains its temperature throughout the system.

4. **Insulating Fittings and Connections:**

   Pay special attention to insulating duct fittings, connections, and other irregular shapes. These areas can be prone to heat loss if not properly insulated.

5. **Consider Insulating Ductwork Internally:**

For existing ducts or situations where external insulation is not feasible, consider internally lining the ducts with insulation. This can be done using materials like duct liners.

6. **Install Radiant Barriers for Outdoor Ducts:**

   If ductwork is exposed to direct sunlight, consider using radiant barriers on the exterior of the ducts to reflect some of the heat.

7. **Provide Mechanical Protection:**

   In areas where ductwork is exposed to potential damage (e.g., mechanical rooms), use protective coverings or shields to safeguard the insulation.

8. **Regular Inspection and Maintenance:**

   Periodically inspect the insulation and ductwork for signs of damage, wear, or moisture accumulation. Address any issues promptly.

9. **Prevent Air Leaks and Seal Ductwork Properly:**

   Use mastic or metal tape to seal any joints or seams in the ductwork. This prevents air leakage and helps maintain the desired temperature.

10. **Consider External Insulation for Outdoor Ducts:**

    If ducts are located in unconditioned spaces or outdoors, ensure they are properly insulated externally to prevent heat loss.

11 **Addressing Condensation Issues:**

   If condensation is a concern, choose insulation materials with a vapor barrier or add a separate vapor barrier layer. Additionally, proper sealing and insulation thickness can help prevent condensation.

Remember that the effectiveness of ductwork insulation depends on factors like the type of insulation material, installation quality, and environmental conditions. It is recommended to consult with insulation professionals or HVAC experts for specific recommendations tailored to your system and environment.

CASE STUDY

In the chilly climate of Delhi, CoolTech Refrigeration Systems tackled persistent condensation challenges within their HVAC systems by implementing insulation ducting in 2020. Partnering with InsulatePro Solutions, the company applied moisture-resistant insulation to the entire ductwork, preventing condensation-related issues such as mould growth and equipment corrosion. The insulation not only improved indoor air quality and operational continuity but also resulted in a remarkable 20% reduction in maintenance costs, extending the lifespan of critical components. Additionally, the insulation ducting enhanced energy efficiency, leading to notable cost savings and positioning CoolTech as a case study in how a strategic approach to insulation can effectively combat condensation issues, ensuring a healthier working environment and long-term operational efficiency.

INSULATING EQUIPMENT AND MACHINERY

In India, insulating equipment and machinery play a crucial role in various industries to ensure safety, efficiency, and compliance with regulatory standards. Insulation must be applied to boilers, reactors, and all such equipment to conserve energy. Here are some common applications of insulating equipment and machinery in different industries:

1. **Power Generation and Distribution:**

   Thermal Insulation: Used in power plants to minimise heat loss in boilers, steam turbines, and pipes. Major shutdowns are common in this sector.

   Electrical Insulation: Insulating materials are used to protect electrical components and workers from electric shock. This is altogether a different topic and will not be covered fully in the book.

2. **Chemical and Petrochemical Industries:**

   Thermal Insulation: Applied to pipes, tanks, reactors, and other equipment to maintain process temperatures and prevent heat loss. This is also the biggest industry for insulation; continuous rate contracts are given to contractors by these large companies.

   Corrosion Protection: Coatings and linings are used to protect against corrosive chemicals. Usually, aluminium cladding is applied, and once rusted, a dedicated paint team repaints it repeatedly.

3. **Oil and Gas Industry:**

   Thermal Insulation: Applied to pipelines, storage tanks, and equipment to maintain the temperature of transported fluids. These pieces of equipment at oil fields are very large, and high temperatures must be maintained in storage tanks.

Fireproofing: Used to protect against the risk of fires in refineries and storage facilities.

4. **Automotive Manufacturing:**

Sound Insulation: Applied to vehicle interiors to reduce noise levels for driver and passenger comfort. Also called acoustic insulation.

Thermal Insulation: Used to regulate temperatures in vehicle components and engine compartments.

5. **Building and Construction:**

Thermal Insulation: Used in residential, commercial, and industrial buildings to conserve energy and maintain indoor comfort.

Sound Insulation: Applied to walls, floors, and ceilings to reduce noise transmission between rooms.

6. **Steel and Metal Industries:**

Thermal Insulation: Applied to furnaces, kilns, and other high-temperature equipment to conserve energy and improve process efficiency.

Vibration Insulation: Used to reduce vibrations in heavy machinery.

7. **Food Processing and Cold Storage:**

Thermal Insulation: Used in refrigeration and cold storage facilities to maintain low temperatures. Used everywhere from dairy to powder; all food grades need it.

Hygienic Insulation: Specialized insulating materials are used in food processing environments to meet sanitary standards.

8. **Textile and Garment Industries:**

Thermal Insulation: Applied in textile dyeing and finishing processes to control temperatures and save energy.

9. **Pharmaceutical and Healthcare:**

   Thermal Insulation: Used in facilities that require controlled temperature environments for drug storage and production.

It is worth noting that the specific types of insulating equipment and machinery used in each industry can vary based on factors such as the type of processes involved, the materials being handled, and the environmental conditions. Additionally, compliance with local and national safety and environmental regulations is a critical consideration in the selection and application of insulating equipment.

3.1 EQUIPMENT SELECTION FOR OPTIMAL INSULATION

Selecting the optimal insulation equipment involves considering various factors related to the specific application, environment, and budget constraints. Here are some steps and considerations for equipment selection for optimal insulation:

1. **Understand the Application:**

   Identify the purpose of insulation (thermal, electrical, sound, etc.) and the specific requirements for the application (e.g., temperature range, voltage, noise reduction goals). Hot/cold/dual insulation might affect the decision.

2. **Determine the Insulation Material:**

   Choose the appropriate insulation material based on its thermal conductivity, electrical resistance, fire resistance, and other relevant properties. Common materials include fiberglass, mineral wool, foam boards, rubber, plastics, and specialised coatings.

3. **Evaluate Environmental Conditions:**

   Consider factors such as moisture exposure, chemical exposure, temperature fluctuations, and potential mechanical stress. Select insulation materials that are compatible with the environmental conditions of the application. If there is too much moisture in the climate, using stainless steel would make more sense.

4. **Consider Regulatory Compliance:**

Ensure that the chosen insulation equipment meets relevant industry standards, building codes, and safety regulations. This may include specific requirements for fire resistance, toxicity, and environmental impact.

5. **Calculate Insulation Thickness:**

Determine the appropriate thickness of insulation needed to achieve the desired level of performance. This may involve conducting heat transfer calculations to optimise energy efficiency. This was explained in detail above.

6. **Select Insulation Form:**

Choose between rolls, batts, boards, blankets, or custom-fit insulation jackets based on the shape and size of the equipment or structure being insulated. Rolls are the most common in industries.

7. **Choose Insulation Accessories:**

Select complementary items like sealants, adhesives, fasteners, and protective coverings to ensure proper installation and long-term effectiveness. These are generally as per engineering requirements; usually, there is not much difference that it makes when it comes to ancillary but still, we need to follow.

8. **Consider Maintenance and Accessibility:**

Assess how easy it will be to access and maintain the insulated components over time. For example, in industrial settings, removable insulation jackets may be preferred for equipment that requires periodic maintenance.

9. **Evaluate Cost and Budget Constraints:**

Balance the initial cost of insulation materials and equipment with the expected energy savings or other benefits over the lifespan of the insulation. A lot of times unethical practices occur during measurements; one should be aware of the same.

10. **Consult with Insulation Experts:**

Seek advice from insulation professionals, engineers, or consultants who have experience in the specific industry or application. They can provide valuable insights and recommendations. You can also consult with my company, Thermal Engineering Projects.

11. **Test and Monitor Performance:**

After installation, conduct tests or measurements to verify that the insulation is performing as expected. This may include thermal imaging, resistance measurements, or sound level assessments. Many testing instruments are available.

12. **Consider Long-Term Durability:**

Choose insulation equipment and materials that have a proven track record of durability and resistance to degradation over time. Consultants with experience in this area can suggest good options, which shall be beneficial.

Remember that each application is unique, and the optimal insulation equipment will vary depending on the specific requirements and conditions. It is important to carefully assess these factors and, if in doubt, seek advice from insulation experts or consult relevant industry standards and guidelines.

CASE STUDY

In Mumbai, EcoHeat Solutions conducted a case study to illustrate the importance of optimal equipment selection for achieving superior insulation in a chemical manufacturing plant. The facility grappled with thermal inefficiencies, prompting EcoHeat to meticulously analyse and select insulation materials and equipment tailored to the specific operational needs. By strategically choosing high-performance insulation materials and advanced equipment, such as thermal imaging systems and energy-efficient HVAC units, the plant experienced a remarkable 25% reduction in energy consumption and a 30% decrease in operational downtimes. The case study highlighted how the thoughtful selection of insulation equipment not only enhanced energy efficiency but also significantly improved overall operational effectiveness, positioning EcoHeat Solutions as a leader in implementing strategic insulation solutions for industrial facilities.

3.2 MACHINE INSULATION: BEST PRACTICES FOR PERFORMANCE ENHANCEMENT

Machine insulation is crucial for maintaining operational efficiency, preventing energy loss, ensuring worker safety, and extending the lifespan of equipment. Many sugar plants perform machine insulation to enhance capability. Here are some best practices for enhancing the performance of machine insulation:

1. **Select the Right Insulation Material:**

    Choose an insulation material that is suitable for the specific application. Consider factors like temperature range, moisture exposure, chemical resistance, and fire safety requirements.

2. **Optimize Insulation Thickness:**

    Determine the appropriate insulation thickness based on factors such as temperature differentials, ambient conditions, and desired energy efficiency. Thicker insulation generally provides better performance, but it's important to strike a balance to avoid over-insulating.

3. **Ensure Proper Installation:**

    Insulation should be installed correctly and securely to prevent gaps, voids, or compression. Pay attention to joints, seams, and connections to ensure a continuous barrier.

4. **Use Vapor Barriers and Sealants:**

    Apply vapor barriers to prevent moisture ingress, which can reduce the effectiveness of insulation. Additionally, use sealants to close gaps and seams in the insulation.

5. **Consider Removable Insulation Jackets:**

   In industrial settings, especially for equipment that requires periodic maintenance, consider using removable insulation jackets. These jackets allow easy access for maintenance while still providing effective insulation.

6. **Protect Insulation from Mechanical Damage:**

   Install protective coverings or shields to safeguard insulation from physical damage caused by impact, vibration, or abrasion.

7. **Implement Fireproofing Measures:**

   In applications where fire safety is a concern, use fire-resistant insulation materials and coatings to provide an additional layer of protection.

8. **Monitor and Replace Damaged Insulation:**

   Regularly inspect insulation for signs of wear, damage, or degradation. Promptly replace any compromised insulation to maintain its effectiveness.

9. **Ensure Proper Ventilation and Airflow:**

   Proper ventilation around insulated components helps prevent the buildup of heat or moisture that could degrade insulation over time.

10. **Consider Insulation Blankets for Complex Shapes:**

    For equipment with irregular shapes or components, consider using custom-made insulation blankets or covers to ensure a snug fit.

11. **Conduct Regular Performance Checks:**

    Monitor the temperature of insulated components to ensure that they are maintaining the desired levels. Use thermal imaging or temperature probes for accurate measurements.

12. **Train and Educate Maintenance Personnel:**

Provide training to maintenance personnel on the importance of proper insulation maintenance and how to identify and address insulation issues.

13. **Document and Keep Records:**

Maintain records of insulation materials used, installation details, and any maintenance or replacement activities. This documentation can be valuable for future reference and planning.

14. **Consider Energy-Efficient Insulation Practices:**

Explore advanced insulation techniques such as reflective coatings, radiant barriers, and aerogel insulation for enhanced energy efficiency.

By following these best practices, you can maximise the performance and effectiveness of machine insulation, leading to improved operational efficiency, energy savings, and overall equipment reliability.

CASE STUDY

In the pharmaceutical manufacturing facility of Bangalore Pharmaceuticals Ltd., a targeted insulation approach was adopted for critical equipment. The case study revealed that this initiative yielded a 20% reduction in energy consumption, translating to considerable savings in operational costs. The improved thermal control resulted in a 30% decrease in equipment downtime, enhancing production efficiency and product quality. The upfront investment in insulation materials demonstrated a swift return on investment, proving that insulation on machinery not only optimises energy usage but also positively impacts overall operational resilience and financial performance for pharmaceutical companies.

SAFETY PROTOCOLS IN INDUSTRIAL INSULATION

Safety protocols in industrial insulation are essential to protect workers, ensure compliance with regulations, and prevent accidents. All companies have different requirements, some being extremely strict and some lenient. There are times when workers are not interested in using safety gear as they are not comfortable with it. Here are some key safety protocols in industrial insulation, outlined briefly:

1. **Personal Protective Equipment (PPE):**

    Workers should wear appropriate PPE, including gloves, safety glasses, hard hats, respiratory protection, and flame-resistant clothing, to protect against hazards. Best of the brands should be used instead of cheap ones as this is to protect one's body part, and this is our moral duty.

2. **Training and Education:**

    Proper training on insulation materials, installation techniques, and safety procedures is crucial for workers to perform their tasks safely. At our company it is a standard practice to train the workers as per our requirements and only after successful completion of training we will make them work for us.

3. **Hazard Identification and Assessment:**

    Conduct thorough risk assessments to identify potential hazards related to insulation work. Address any identified risks before work begins. This is part of training and should be taught to workers.

4. **Worksite Preparation:**

Ensure the work area is clean, organized, and free of clutter. Use signage to designate work zones and warn of potential hazards. A workshop shall be created for the ease of this, it would be easier for the workers as well to maintain and keep it clean.

5. **Proper Material Handling:**

Train workers on the safe handling, storage, and transportation of insulation materials to prevent accidents and injuries. Materials like aluminium cladding are very expensive; aluminium cladding is the layer of aluminium added above the insulation material. It is added for various reasons, including beautification, safety, UV resistance, protection, etc. This cladding sums up a large amount; we must handle it carefully as this is a thing margin business. If the material gets damaged, we might not be able to use it as it will lose its properties.

6. **Fall Protection:**

Implement fall protection measures for work conducted at heights or on elevated surfaces. This may include guardrails, safety harnesses, or elevated work platforms. Workers shall be trained to work over scaffolding.

7. **Electrical Safety:**

Follow proper lockout/tagout procedures. These are the steps that workers are instructed on in case of any unforeseen events. The point is that manufacturing plants do not shut down, and regular maintenance is performed at all times. There can be a boiler or any other equipment that throws away some chemicals or something at the worker. These procedures are to be followed then. Every company has different procedures for working near electrical equipment. Use insulated tools and equipment for electrical insulation tasks.

8. **Fire Safety:**

   Follow fire safety protocols, including using fire-resistant insulation materials and having firefighting equipment readily available. Conduct hot work procedures safely. Every company will have their own site rules, and workers shall adhere to them anyhow.

9. **Respiratory Protection:**

   Provide respiratory protection when working with materials that generate dust, fumes, or particulate matter. The mask should be mandatory, as mentioned above.

10. **Ventilation:**

    Ensure adequate ventilation in confined spaces to prevent the buildup of hazardous gases or vapours. Timely breaks shall be given to workers so that it ensures higher productivity as well as they can freshen up their mind.

11. **Confined Space Safety:**

    Follow specific protocols when working in confined spaces, including proper ventilation, atmospheric testing, and having a rescue plan in place.

12. **Tool and Equipment Safety:**

    Inspect and maintain tools and equipment regularly to ensure they are in good working condition. Provide proper training on tool use and safety. Regular tool examination and calibration should be done and thoroughly checked by quality control.

13. **Emergency Response and First Aid:**

    Have a well-defined emergency response plan in case of accidents or injuries. Provide training in first aid and ensure access to first aid supplies. Having first aid supplies at the site is mandatory by rule now as passed in the courts of India.

14. **Communication and Coordination:**

Establish clear communication channels between workers, supervisors, and safety personnel. Encourage open dialogue about safety concerns. A clear hierarchy shall be maintained with organisation structure.

15. **Incident Reporting and Investigation:**

Establish a reporting system for near misses, accidents, and incidents. Conduct thorough investigations to identify root causes and implement corrective actions.

16. **Regular Safety Audits and Inspections:**

Conduct routine inspections of work areas and equipment to identify and rectify potential safety hazards. A quality control engineer should timely visit different sites and observe the quality of work and the safety that is followed. A report shall be made regularly.

17. **Compliance with Regulations:**

Ensure compliance with local, state, and national safety regulations and standards applicable to insulation work.

By adhering to these safety protocols, industrial insulation projects can be completed with a reduced risk of accidents or injuries, creating a safer work environment for all involved.

CASE STUDY

In the heart of the edible oil industry in Mumbai, GoldenOils Ltd. implemented a strategic insulation project on their processing equipment. Safety took centre stage during this initiative, with a meticulous focus on preventing potential hazards associated with hot surfaces. The insulation measures not only ensured the safety of the plant personnel but also contributed to an impressive 20% reduction in energy consumption. By combining safety protocols with insulation, GoldenOils achieved a seamless production process, minimizing downtime and enhancing overall operational efficiency. This case study illustrates the synergy between safety considerations and insulation initiatives in the edible oil industry, demonstrating tangible benefits in terms of personnel well-being and operational excellence.

4.1 FIRE SAFETY AND FLAME-RETARDANT INSULATION

Fire safety and the use of flame-retardant insulation are critical aspects of building design and industrial applications. Here are some key considerations for fire safety and flame-retardant insulation:

Fire Safety:

1. Building Codes and Standards:

Adhere to local and national building codes and standards that specify requirements for fire safety in construction.

2. Fire Risk Assessment:

Conduct a thorough assessment of potential fire risks in the building or industrial facility. Identify areas where fire hazards may be present.

3. Fire Suppression Systems:

Install and maintain fire suppression systems, such as sprinklers and fire extinguishers, to quickly respond to fires and minimise damage.

4. Emergency Exits and Evacuation Plans:

Ensure that the building has clearly marked emergency exits and establish evacuation plans to safely evacuate occupants in the event of a fire.

5. Smoke Detectors and Alarms:

Install smoke detectors and fire alarms to provide early warning of a fire, allowing occupants to evacuate promptly.

6. Fire-Resistant Construction Materials:

Use fire-resistant materials in construction, including fire-rated walls, ceilings, and floors, to contain and prevent the spread of fires.

FLAME-RETARDANT INSULATION:

1. **Selection of Flame-Retardant Materials:**

   Choose insulation materials that are specifically designed to be flame-retardant or have been treated with flame-retardant additives.

2. **Testing and Certification:**

   Ensure that the chosen insulation materials have been tested and certified for their flame-retardant properties by reputable testing agencies.

3. **Compliance with Standards:**

   Use insulation materials that comply with industry-specific fire safety standards and building codes.

4. **Proper Installation:**

   Follow manufacturer guidelines and industry best practices for the installation of flame-retardant insulation. Ensure that the insulation is properly fitted and sealed to prevent gaps or voids.

5. **Seal Penetrations and Joints:**

   Seal any penetrations, joints, or openings in the insulation to maintain its fire-resistant properties and prevent the spread of flames or smoke.

6. **Regular Inspection and Maintenance:**

   Inspect flame-retardant insulation regularly to ensure that it remains in good condition and has not been damaged or compromised.

7. **Compatibility with Other Materials:**

   Ensure that flame-retardant insulation materials are compatible with other components and materials used in the construction or industrial process.

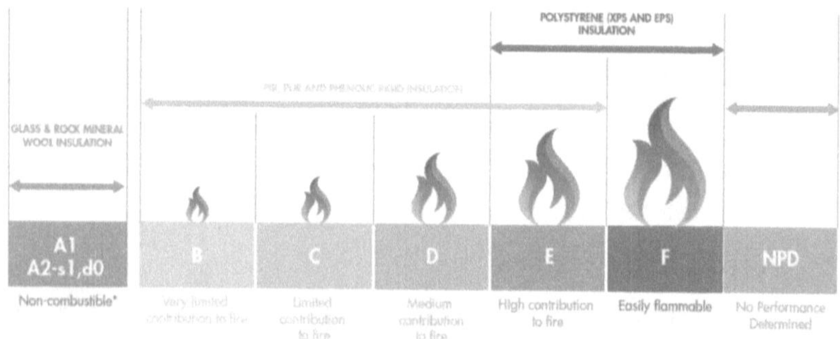

8. **Training and Awareness:**

    Provide training to workers, maintenance personnel, and occupants about the importance of flame-retardant insulation and fire safety measures.

9. **Documentation and Record-Keeping:**

    Maintain records of the type of flame-retardant insulation used, installation details, and any maintenance or replacement activities.

By incorporating flame-retardant insulation and adhering to fire safety practices, you can help mitigate the risk of fires and enhance the safety of occupants in buildings or industrial facilities. It's important to work with qualified professionals and ensure that all materials and systems meet applicable safety standards and regulations.

CASE STUDY:

In the urban landscape of Delhi, Coromandel Industries, a leading manufacturer of chemical products, conducted a fire safety case study to assess where fires might start and if a plan is needed to stop them in a timely manner. The fire safety study was conducted following the implementation of advanced insulation measures in their production facility. Facing heightened risks due to the nature of their operations, Coromandel prioritised fire safety during the insulation project, incorporating fire-resistant materials and designing insulation layouts to mitigate potential fire hazards. The case study revealed that the strategic integration of fire-safe insulation not only prevented fire incidents but also minimised the extent of damage in case of accidental fires. Through this initiative, Coromandel achieved a commendable 30% reduction in fire-related risks, fostering a safer working environment and exemplifying the crucial role of fire safety considerations in insulation projects within industries with elevated fire hazards.

4.2 SAFETY GEARS FOR INSULATION

When working with insulation materials, it's crucial to prioritise safety; otherwise, it may cause serious health problems. Here are some recommended safety gear and equipment for insulation work:

1. **Personal Protective Equipment (PPE):**

   Safety Glasses or Goggles: To protect the eyes from dust, fibres, and potential flying debris.

   Dust Mask or Respirator: Especially when handling loose-fill or blown-in insulation that can generate dust particles.

   Gloves: Provide hand protection against skin irritation, cuts, and abrasions. Choose gloves appropriate for the type of insulation material.

   Long-Sleeved Shirt and Pants: To prevent direct skin contact with insulation fibres or materials that may cause irritation. The best option is a boiler suit.

2. **Footwear:**

   Sturdy, closed-toe shoes or work boots with non-slip soles to provide support, prevent slips, and to protect against falling objects. The image is a very universal design for the same.

3. **Head Protection:**

Hard Hat: Especially when working in areas where there's a risk of falling objects or overhead hazards. A good-quality helmet is essential.

4. **Hearing Protection:**

Ear Plugs or Ear Muffs: Important when working in noisy environments, such as industrial settings.

5. **Insulated Tools:**

Tools with insulated handles, especially if working near electrical components, to prevent the risk of electric shock.

6. **First Aid Kit:**

Have a well-stocked first aid kit readily available in case of minor injuries or accidents. Minor injuries are normal and regular at these types of job. Our focus should be to avoid anything major.

7. **Fire Extinguisher:**

Especially important when working with flammable insulation materials. Ensure that workers know how to use it.

Remember that the specific safety gear required may vary depending on the type of insulation material and the specific conditions of the work environment. Always follow manufacturer recommendations and industry best practices for safety

CASE STUDY

In the industrial city of Ahmedabad, Gujarat, Knauf Insulation conducted a case study highlighting the instrumental role of safety gear for insulation workers during a complex project at a petrochemical facility. The insulation crew was equipped with specialised personal protective equipment, including fire-resistant coveralls, safety helmets, and respiratory protection. The study revealed that the use of safety gear not only protected workers from potential thermal and chemical hazards but also contributed to a 25% reduction in project completion time due to increased worker confidence and efficiency. The incident-free completion of the project underscored the significance of prioritising safety gear, showcasing how it not only ensures worker well-being but also positively impacts the overall success and timeline of insulation projects in Gujarat's industrial sector.

Chapter V

SUSTAINABILITY AND ENVIRONMENTAL IMPACT

Industrial insulation can have a significant positive impact on sustainability and the environment in several ways:

1. **Energy Efficiency and Reduced Emissions:**

   Insulating industrial equipment, pipes, and structures helps to minimise heat loss or gain. This leads to reduced energy consumption, lower greenhouse gas emissions, and a smaller carbon footprint. Major companies are willing to become carbon neutral in the coming years, and in such cases, insulation will be the best option for them.

2. **Resource Conservation:**

   By improving energy efficiency, insulation reduces the need for extracting, processing, and transporting raw materials for energy production. This conserves natural resources and reduces the environmental impact associated with resource extraction.

3. **Waste Reduction:**

   Properly installed and maintained insulation can extend the lifespan of equipment and structures, reducing the need for frequent replacements. This leads to less waste generation and lower demand for new materials. Many insulation materials are re-used on site; this is a very common practice.

4. **Air Quality Improvement:**

   Insulation can help prevent the release of pollutants and emissions from industrial processes into the atmosphere. This contributes to better air quality and reduces health risks for nearby communities. There are specific targets set by the government for these corporate companies, and they must stay below the limit.

5. **Mitigation of Heat Island Effect:**

In urban areas, large industrial facilities can contribute to the "urban heat island" effect. Insulating buildings and equipment can help regulate temperatures and reduce the impact of this phenomenon. Godrej Industries was one of the early adopters of this practice in India.

6. **Water Conservation:**

Insulation can help maintain stable temperatures in processes that use water, reducing the need for excess water to compensate for heat losses.

7. **Reduction of Noise Pollution:**

Certain types of insulation materials can help dampen noise levels, making industrial operations less disruptive to surrounding communities.

8. **Compliance with Environmental Regulations:**

Many regions have regulations in place to limit emissions and energy consumption in industrial operations. Proper insulation helps industries meet these regulatory requirements.

9. **Improved Indoor Environmental Quality (IEQ):**

Insulation can contribute to better indoor air quality by preventing the infiltration of outdoor pollutants and reducing the potential for condensation and mould growth.

10. **Enhanced Resilience to Climate Change:**

Insulated facilities are better equipped to handle extreme temperatures and weather events, making them more resilient in the face of climate change impacts.

11. **Sustainable Material Choices:**

Choosing insulation materials made from recycled or renewable resources, or those with low environmental impact, can further enhance the sustainability of industrial insulation projects.

12. Life Cycle Assessment (LCA):

Conducting a life cycle assessment of insulation materials and systems helps evaluate their environmental impact over their entire lifespan, including production, installation, use, and disposal.

It's important to note that the overall sustainability and environmental impact of industrial insulation can vary depending on factors like the specific materials used, installation practices, and the context of the application. Therefore, careful consideration and selection of insulation materials and installation techniques are crucial to achieving the greatest positive environmental outcomes.

CASE STUDY

In Pune's environmentally conscious industrial landscape, Praj Industries conducted a case study to evaluate the ecological impact of insulation in their operations. Commencing in 2019, the company strategically insulated critical components such as boilers and pipelines, using eco-friendly materials. The results were profound, with a 30% reduction in overall energy consumption, leading to a substantial decrease in carbon emissions. Beyond the immediate financial gains from reduced energy costs, the case study illustrated that insulation, when implemented thoughtfully, can serve as a powerful tool in mitigating industrial contributions to climate change, highlighting the pivotal role of insulation in fostering environmental sustainability within manufacturing practices.

V.1 NOISE REDUCTION STRATEGIES AND MATERIALS FOR IMPROVED WORK ENVIRONMENT.

Reducing noise in an industrial setting is crucial for creating a safer and more comfortable work environment. Here are some noise reduction strategies and materials that can be employed in conjunction with industrial insulation:

1. **Sound Absorption Materials:**

    Acoustic Panels and Tiles: Install acoustic panels or tiles on walls and ceilings to absorb sound waves and reduce reverberation. Many theatres, offices, and road touch offices are doing this to avoid sound waves travelling too fast and affecting them.

    Mineral Wool and Acoustic Foam: These materials are effective at absorbing sound and can be used in wall cavities, ceilings, and partitions. This is a standard practice in America; people usually do this while building their houses.

2. **Enclosures and Barriers:**

    Enclosures: Construct enclosures around noisy equipment to contain and mitigate the spread of noise.

    Sound Barrier Walls: Erect barriers or walls made of sound-absorbing materials to block noise transmission to neighbouring areas. This is most common in companies where the corporate office is adjacent to the plant where manufacturing happens.

3. **Vibration Isolation:**

    Use vibration isolation mounts or pads under machinery and equipment to reduce the transmission of vibrations that generate noise.

4. **Damping Materials:**

    Apply damping materials like damping sheets or coatings to machinery surfaces to reduce the generation of structural-borne noise. Dampers are a perfect example of this. Most companies do have dampers in their plants.

5. **Absorptive Ceilings:**

Install acoustic ceiling tiles or baffles to absorb sound and reduce noise levels in large industrial spaces.

6. **Noise-Canceling Technologies:**

Implement active noise control systems that use microphones and speakers to generate sound waves that cancel out unwanted noise. There are also large industrial equipment made these days that can cancel noise and avoid disturbances.

7. **Mufflers and Silencers:**

Install mufflers or silencers on exhaust systems, ventilation ducts, and pneumatic equipment (i.e. tools that play an important role in air control) to reduce noise emissions.

8. **Proper Maintenance and Lubrication:**

Regularly maintain and lubricate machinery to reduce friction and minimise noise generated during operation.

9. **Workstation Design:**

Arrange workstations to minimise noise exposure for employees and provide acoustic shielding or barriers where needed.

10. **Training and Awareness:**

Educate employees on the importance of hearing protection and noise-reduction practices, and provide appropriate training on equipment operation.

11. **Noise Monitoring and Assessment:**

Conduct regular noise assessments to identify areas with high noise levels and implement targeted solutions. A decibel meter is a suitable equipment for this; it is now present in smartwatches as well, notifying users of high volumes.

12. **Use of Sound Masking:**

   Implement sound masking systems that emit background noise to mask or cover up unwanted sounds.

13. **Selective Insulation:**

Insulate walls, floors, and ceilings with sound-absorbing materials like acoustic panels to contain and reduce noise levels within a specific area.

14. **Compliance with Regulations:**

   Ensure compliance with local and national regulations regarding permissible noise levels in industrial settings.

15. **Consult with Acoustic Engineers:**

   Engage with acoustic engineers or consultants who specialise in noise control for expert advice and tailored solutions.

By combining these strategies with appropriate insulation materials and techniques, you can create a more comfortable and productive work environment while reducing the risk of noise-related health issues for employees. We do not really specialise in acoustic insulation but have done a few jobs for the same.

CASE STUDY

In the vibrant industrial hub of Bangalore, Harmony Dynamics, a call centre facility, implemented a case study focusing on the positive effects of acoustic insulation in their open office environment. Recognising the detrimental impact of high noise levels on employee concentration and well-being, the company introduced comprehensive acoustic insulation measures in 2019. The results were evident, showcasing a 25% reduction in ambient noise, leading to increased employee satisfaction, improved focus, and a notable decrease in stress levels. This case study underscores how strategic acoustic insulation not only contributes to a more tranquil work environment but also positively impacts employee performance and satisfaction in the fast-paced setting of a call centre.

V.II LIFE CYCLE ASSESSMENT AND ENVIRONMENTAL CONSIDERATION

Life Cycle Assessment (LCA) is a comprehensive methodology used to evaluate the environmental impacts of a product, process, or service throughout its entire life cycle, from raw material extraction to disposal. When applied to industrial insulation, LCA helps assess the environmental considerations associated with its production, installation, use, and eventual end-of-life.

Here are key points to consider in a Life Cycle Assessment of industrial insulation:

1. **Raw Material Extraction and Production:**

    Assess the environmental impact of sourcing raw materials for insulation production. Consider factors like energy use, resource depletion, and emissions associated with material extraction and manufacturing.

2. **Manufacturing Process:**

    Evaluate the energy consumption, emissions, and waste generated during the production of insulation materials. Compare different manufacturing techniques and technologies for their environmental performance.

3. **Transportation and Distribution:**

    Analyse the environmental impacts of transporting insulation materials from production facilities to installation sites. Consider transportation modes, distances, and associated emissions.

4. **Installation and Use:**

    Consider the energy and resource consumption during the installation process. Evaluate the insulation's effectiveness in reducing energy consumption and emissions in the operational phase of the facility.

5. **Energy Efficiency and Emissions Reduction:**

Assess the insulation's impact on energy efficiency, including its ability to reduce heating or cooling needs. Calculate the corresponding reduction in greenhouse gas emissions over the facility's operational life.

6. **Durability and Maintenance:**

Evaluate the longevity and durability of the insulation material. Consider maintenance requirements and the need for replacements or repairs over time.

7. **End-of-Life and Disposal:**

Analyse the environmental impact of disposing of or recycling insulation materials at the end of their useful life. Consider factors like recyclability, landfill impact, and potential for reusing materials.

8. **Comparative Analysis:**

Compare the environmental performance of different insulation materials and installation methods. This helps identify the most sustainable options for specific applications.

9. **Environmental Considerations:**

Consider specific environmental factors, such as water usage, emissions of pollutants, and impacts on biodiversity, that may be relevant to the insulation material or installation process.

10. **Local and Regional Considerations:**

Take into account regional differences in energy sources, climate conditions, and regulatory frameworks that may influence the environmental impact of insulation.

11. **Life Cycle Cost Analysis (LCCA):**

Complement LCA with a Life Cycle Cost Analysis to consider both environmental and economic aspects, helping identify solutions that offer the best balance between sustainability and cost-effectiveness.

By conducting a thorough Life Cycle Assessment of industrial insulation, it is possible to make informed decisions that promote environmentally responsible practices and minimise the overall environmental footprint of insulation materials and systems.

CASE STUDY

In Vadodara, Sustainable Homes Ltd. conducted a pioneering case study focused on the life cycle and environmental impacts of insulation in their residential construction projects, commencing in 2020. The study systematically evaluated insulation materials, considering their entire life cycle from cradle to grave. By emphasising the use of materials with lower embodied energy and reduced environmental impact, Sustainable Homes achieved a remarkable 25% reduction in the overall carbon footprint of their buildings. This case study serves as a testament to how conscientious insulation choices can significantly contribute to sustainable construction practices, fostering environmentally responsible residential developments and providing valuable insights for the broader construction industry.

MAINTENANCE, REPAIR AND LONGEVITY

Maintaining and repairing industrial insulation is crucial for ensuring its effectiveness and longevity. Here are some key considerations for maintenance, repair, and enhancing the longevity of industrial insulation:

1. **Regular Inspection:**

   Conduct routine inspections to identify any signs of wear, damage, or degradation in the insulation. Look for areas with missing or displaced insulation, as well as signs of moisture or deterioration. If ignored, this will lead to energy loss, and there will be no point in insulation then. Routine checks should be conducted, and if any damage is found, it should be resolved immediately.

2. **Prompt Repairs:**

   Address any identified issues promptly. Repair or replace damaged or deteriorated insulation to maintain its effectiveness. This is why big companies always have an insulation contractor like us to repair any damages on site, so that it does not affect the company's productivity.

3. **Weatherproofing and Sealing:**

   Ensure that insulation is properly sealed to prevent the intrusion of moisture, air, or contaminants. Apply weatherproofing materials like wool, paint, cement, etc., or coatings where necessary. Many states in India have a lot of moisture in the air, which boosts corrosion on equipment, pipelines, etc.

4. **Protection from Mechanical Damage:**

Install protective coverings or shields to safeguard insulation from physical damage caused by impact, vibration, or abrasion. This is especially important in high-traffic areas.

5. **Removable Insulation Jackets:**

Consider using removable insulation jackets for equipment that requires periodic maintenance. These jackets allow easy access for inspection and repairs without compromising insulation effectiveness. Very few companies use this, as it is not as cost-effective as it should be.

6. **Repairing Joints and Seams:**

Inspect and repair joints, seams, and connections to ensure that the insulation forms a continuous barrier. Use appropriate sealants or adhesives. Every material will react differently to different adhesives, so correct materials should be used to seal the material. If one layer is not sufficient, use two layers to seal it perfectly.

7. **Insulation Blankets for Complex Shapes:**

For equipment with irregular shapes or components, consider using custom-made insulation blankets or covers to ensure a snug fit and complete coverage. This takes a long time to be delivered, so the standard practice is to get the material in wool form and seal it, as wool form can fit into any shape.

8. **Preventing Corrosion:**

Inspect for signs of corrosion on pipes or equipment. Addressing corrosion promptly can help prevent further damage to the insulation. As mentioned above, this is very common in the climatic conditions present in India.

9. **Fireproofing Measures:**

If fire safety is a concern, ensure that fire-resistant insulation materials and coatings are in place to provide an additional layer of protection.

10. **Monitoring and Testing:**

Implement regular testing and monitoring of insulation performance. This may include thermal imaging, resistance measurements, or sound level assessments.

11. **Cleaning and Maintenance of HVAC Systems:**

Regularly clean and maintain HVAC systems to ensure that air ducts and associated insulation remain in good condition. This will increase the product standard.

12. **Documenting Repairs and Maintenance:**

Keep records of all repairs, maintenance activities, and replacements related to industrial insulation. This documentation helps track the history of the insulation system. It is necessary to understand the quality of work that is done. If a single team is having these issues repeatedly, consider replacing them.

13. **Training and Education:**

Provide training to maintenance personnel on the importance of proper insulation maintenance and how to identify and address insulation issues. Having a trained insulation team is crucial. Their training and experience will help the company increase the efficiency and productivity of their plants. This will also save costs and energy and help achieve carbon neutrality sooner.

14. **Consideration of Environmental Conditions:**

Ensure that insulation materials are compatible with the environmental conditions of the application. For example, choose materials that are resistant to moisture or chemicals if needed.

By following these practices, you can maximise the performance and longevity of industrial insulation, leading to improved operational efficiency and energy savings. Regular maintenance and prompt repairs are key to ensuring that insulation continues to provide effective thermal, acoustic, and safety benefits over time.

CASE STUDY:

In the industrial complex of Godrej Industries Ltd. in Mumbai, a strategic case study was conducted on the proactive maintenance of insulation systems, initiated in 2018. Godrej Industries implemented a comprehensive approach involving regular inspections, timely repairs, and the adoption of advanced insulation technologies across their manufacturing processes. The study revealed impressive outcomes, including a 20% reduction in energy consumption and a notable 25% decrease in maintenance costs over the course of two years. The proactive maintenance strategy not only optimised the efficiency of critical equipment but also contributed to sustainable operations. This case study illustrates how Godrej Industries, through meticulous insulation maintenance, achieved significant energy savings and cost-efficiency, exemplifying best practices for insulation management within large-scale industrial operations.

6.1 ASSESSING AND ADDRESSING WEAR AND TEAR IN INDUSTRIAL INSULATION

Assessing and addressing wear and tear in industrial insulation is crucial for maintaining its effectiveness and ensuring safety. If not taken care of, it may result in energy loss and increased production costs for the company. Here are steps you can take to assess and address wear and tear:

1. **Regular Inspections:**

    Conduct routine inspections of the insulation system. This should be done at regular intervals to identify any signs of wear, damage, or deterioration. The quality control manager should have regular visits to the site and check the quality of work done by workers. This includes everything from checking how well it is sealed to checking for moisture. This job is mandatory, and issues should be resolved at the earliest.

2. **Visual Examination:**

    Visually inspect the insulation for visible signs of wear and tear, such as cracks, gaps, tears, or areas with missing insulation. This should also be done by a quality inspector, or the site supervisor should be given the authority to do these small jobs. This is necessary to conserve energy and keep the work going.

3. **Check for Water Damage:**

    Look for signs of water damage, including discolouration, warping, or softening of the insulation material. Address any leaks or sources of moisture promptly. There are fireproof materials but not waterproof ones. So, any signs of water or moisture should be considered dangerous, and the insulation should be refixed immediately.

4. **Assess for Physical Damage:**

    Inspect for any physical damage caused by impact, vibration, or abrasion. Pay close attention to areas near moving parts or high-traffic zones. As mentioned above, action should be taken by the quality head or site supervisor once they assess the situation. Waiting in such scenarios may reduce profitability (although marginally, it does affect the overall margin).

5. **Evaluate Insulation Thickness:**

    Measure the thickness of the insulation. Over time, insulation may compress or degrade, reducing its effectiveness. If needed, consider adding additional insulation to maintain the desired thickness. This is explained in the previous chapters. Using those concepts, one should evaluate the required thickness and cross-check the actual thickness. There will be times when workers may have used less thick material. Thus, due diligence is required.

6. **Check Seals and Joints:**

    Examine joints, seams, and connections in the insulation system. Ensure that they are properly sealed to prevent gaps or voids. Proper due diligence techniques should be used here to ensure proper sealing. The quality control engineer should randomly check 5 joints out of 100; this random picking is the only way to understand the situation, as you cannot open all 100 joints and reseal them.

7. **Monitor for Corrosion:**

    Inspect pipes or equipment for signs of corrosion. Corrosion can lead to the deterioration of both the insulation and the underlying structure. Corrosion is very dangerous and should be addressed immediately. If ignored, it will damage the underlying structure such as heaters, boilers, pipelines, etc. To avoid this, corrosion should be monitored closely, and immediate action should be taken.

8. **Use Non-Destructive Testing (NDT) Techniques:**

    Consider employing NDT methods like ultrasound or thermal imaging to assess the condition of the insulation without causing further damage. This is an expensive process and is rather uncommon in India.

9. **Identify Potential Hotspots:**

Use thermal imaging or temperature probes to identify areas where insulation may be failing to maintain desired temperatures. These should be installed in cameras present at the site to monitor heat or any form of energy.

10. **Conduct Materials Testing:**

If possible, conduct testing on insulation samples to assess properties like thermal conductivity, density, and moisture resistance. Agencies provide these testing instruments and sell them. These instruments help check various factors.

11. **Addressing Wear and Tear:**

For minor damage, consider repairing or patching affected areas using appropriate insulation materials and sealants. There are methods to do so, but it may depend on the situation; there is no standard guidebook available.

12. **Replacement of Damaged Sections:**

If wear and tear are extensive or if the insulation material has significantly degraded, it may be necessary to replace entire sections. It should be thoroughly checked, and before the insulation causes any problems to the final product or functionality of the plant, it should be replaced immediately. Such problems should be avoided.

13. **Reinforcement or Protective Measures:**

Consider implementing measures to protect insulation from further wear and tear. This may include adding shields, covers, or guards in vulnerable areas. You can also refix the insulation, meaning remove the current insulation, assess if it can be reused. If it can be reused, refix it; otherwise, use new material and fix it properly again.

14. **Reassessment of Environmental Conditions:**

    If the environment or operational conditions have changed, reassess the suitability of the current insulation material. It may be necessary to upgrade or replace it with a more appropriate material.

15. **Documentation and Record-Keeping:**

    Maintain records of inspections, assessments, and any repairs or replacements performed. This documentation is valuable for tracking the history of the insulation system. Every task done on site should be recorded. This will help identify which segments have the majority of faults, allowing necessary actions to be taken.

By regularly assessing and addressing wear and tear, you can extend the lifespan of industrial insulation, maintain its effectiveness, and ensure the safety and efficiency of your operations. Prompt action in response to identified issues is key to preventing further damage and preserving the integrity of the insulation system.

CASE STUDY:

In the industrial domain of VVF Ltd., a global specialty chemical and personal care product manufacturer based in Mumbai, a focused case study was conducted to address and manage the wear and tear of insulation systems, commencing in 2020. VVF implemented a rigorous maintenance strategy, encompassing routine inspections, timely repairs, and the incorporation of robust insulation materials to combat wear-related challenges. The study showcased tangible outcomes, including a commendable 15% reduction in heat loss and a 20% decrease in equipment downtime over the subsequent two years. By proactively addressing wear and tear in insulation systems, VVF demonstrated an effective approach to sustaining energy efficiency and operational resilience, providing valuable insights for industrial enterprises facing similar challenges.

6.2 EXTENDING THE LIFESPAN OF INSULATION: RE-PAIR AND REPLACEMENT TECHNIQUES

Extending the lifespan of insulation is crucial for maintaining its effectiveness and maximising its benefits. Here are some repair and replacement techniques to consider:

REPAIR TECHNIQUES:

1. **Patch and Seal:**

   For small areas of damage or wear, patching with compatible insulation materials and sealing with appropriate sealants can effectively address the issue.

2. **Reinforce with Protective Covers:**

   Install protective covers or shields in high-traffic areas or places prone to mechanical damage. This helps prevent further wear and tear.

3. **Add Additional Insulation:**

   If the existing insulation has become compressed or degraded, consider adding supplementary layers to restore the desired thickness.

4. **Seal Joints and Seams:**

   Inspect and repair joints, seams, and connections to ensure a continuous insulation barrier. Use compatible sealants or adhesives for the material.

5. **Apply Weatherproofing Coatings:**

   Use weatherproofing coatings to protect insulation from moisture, contaminants, and environmental exposure.

6. **Reposition or Reattach:**

   If insulation has shifted or become detached, reposition and secure it to ensure proper coverage and effectiveness.

7. **Utilise Removable Insulation Jackets:**

   Install removable insulation jackets in areas where regular access is needed for maintenance. These jackets allow easy removal and reinstallation.

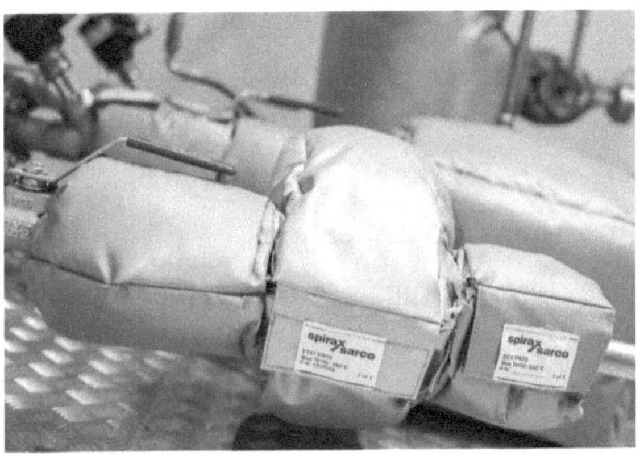

REPLACEMENT TECHNIQUES:

1. **Complete Replacement:**

   In cases of extensive damage, degradation, or inefficacy, a full replacement of the insulation may be necessary.

2. **Upgrade to Higher-Performance Materials:**

   Consider replacing older or less efficient insulation materials with newer, high-performance options that offer better thermal or acoustic properties.

3. **Reevaluate Environmental Conditions:**

   If the operational conditions or environment have changed since the initial installation, reassess the suitability of the current insulation material and consider replacement if needed.

4. **Choose Durable and Long-Lasting Materials:**

   When replacing insulation, select materials like rockwool known for their durability, resistance to wear, and longevity.

5. **Consider Insulation Blankets or Custom Covers:**

For complex or irregularly shaped equipment, consider using custom-made insulation blankets or covers to ensure a snug fit and complete coverage.

6. **Upgrade Fire-Resistant Insulation:**

If fire safety is a concern, consider upgrading to insulation materials that offer enhanced fire resistance and protection.

7. **Best Practices for Both Repair and Replacement:**

Conduct Thorough Inspections:

Before deciding on repair or replacement, conduct detailed inspections to accurately assess the condition and extent of damage.

8. **Choose Compatible Materials:**

Ensure that any repair or replacement materials are compatible with the existing insulation and the environment they will be exposed to.

9. Follow Manufacturer Guidelines:

Adhere to the manufacturer's recommendations and best practices for installation, repair, and replacement of insulation materials.

10. Document and Track Maintenance:

Keep records of all repair and replacement activities, including dates, materials used, and any additional steps taken.

By implementing these repair and replacement techniques, you can effectively extend the lifespan of insulation and maintain its performance over time. Regular maintenance and timely interventions are key to preserving the integrity and effectiveness of the insulation system.

CASE STUDY

In the chemical manufacturing sector, Navin Fluorine International Ltd. undertook a strategic case study in 2020 to expand the lifespan of insulation systems within their production facilities. Recognising the critical role of insulation in energy conservation and operational efficiency, the study focused on proactive maintenance measures, including regular inspections, targeted repairs, and the utilisation of high-quality insulation materials designed to withstand harsh chemical environments. Navin Fluorine also implemented advanced monitoring technologies to detect potential issues early and facilitate prompt interventions. The outcomes were significant, with a commendable 25% extension in the operational longevity of insulation systems observed over a three-year period. This case study underscores Navin Fluorine's commitment to sustainable manufacturing practices and highlights the importance of proactive insulation maintenance in optimising operational performance and resource utilisation within the chemical industry.

Chapter VII

COMPLIANCE WITH CODES AND REGULATIONS

Compliance with codes and regulations is crucial in Indian industries to ensure safety, environmental protection, and overall operational integrity. Here are some key aspects of compliance with codes and regulations in Indian industries:

1. INDUSTRIAL SAFETY:

Factory Act and Rules: Indian industries must comply with the Factories Act, 1948, and its associated rules. These regulations cover aspects such as health, safety, welfare, working hours, and employment conditions. There are also additional rules to be followed, which may differ from company to company.

Occupational Safety and Health Standards: Industries are required to adhere to occupational safety and health standards set by regulatory authorities like the Directorate General Factory Advice Service and Labour Institutes (DGFASLI). Different companies may have varying health and safety standards, as each company defines its own basic safety and health standards. Workers must comply with company rules and take necessary actions.

2. ENVIRONMENTAL COMPLIANCE:

Environmental Protection Acts: Industries must comply with environmental protection acts, including the Water (Prevention and Control of Pollution) Act, 1974, and the Air (Prevention and Control of Pollution) Act, 1981. The plant head should be aware of these acts, and everyone working in the plant should be informed; if not, they should be trained for unforeseen circumstances and the appropriate course of action.

Consent to Operate: Industries need to obtain and maintain valid "Consent to Operate" from the State Pollution Control Boards (SPCBs) or Pollution Control Committees (PCCs) to ensure compliance with environmental standards. This may vary from state to state in India. Each state has its own rules and regulations, which companies must adhere to.

Waste Management: Industries must manage and dispose of hazardous and non-hazardous waste in accordance with the Hazardous and Other Wastes (Management and Transboundary Movement) Rules, 2016. These rules have become stricter in states like Maharashtra, Gujarat, and Andhra Pradesh due to difficulties in waste storage and increasing pollution concerns.

3. FIRE SAFETY COMPLIANCE:

National Building Code (NBC): Compliance with the National Building Code of India, which includes fire safety standards, is essential for ensuring the safe construction and operation of industrial facilities. Many insulation materials are fireproof to a great extent.

Fire Safety Certificates: Obtaining and renewing fire safety certificates from local fire departments is mandatory for industries to operate. This must be done every two years; otherwise, the fire department will not take responsibility for any fire incidents. Numerous rules and regulations must be followed under fire safety compliance, as it involves life-threatening situations if not taken seriously.

4. ELECTRICAL SAFETY:

Indian Electricity Rules: Adherence to the Indian Electricity Rules, which govern electrical installations and equipment, is vital to ensure electrical safety in industrial settings. Proper checking is also mandatory. It is advised to have a team of electricians on-site so they can regularly check and fix anything broken immediately.

5. LABOUR LAWS:

Minimum Wages Act: Industries must comply with the Minimum Wages Act, 1948, to ensure fair remuneration for labour. Our company, being a service-intensive business, must comply with this act. Each state has a different minimum wage rate for every type of worker. At the worker level, there are broadly two types: skilled and unskilled, with different wage rates. There is usually a significant 30% difference.

Payment of Bonus Act: Compliance with the Payment of Bonus Act, 1965, is necessary for providing statutory bonuses to eligible employees. Our company, being service-intensive, must comply with this act. It requires companies to provide bonuses to workers at any time of the year, but it is compulsory. Major companies typically distribute bonuses during Diwali, as it is the most widely celebrated Hindu festival in India.

6. BUILDING AND CONSTRUCTION CODES:

Local Building Codes: Industries must comply with local building codes and regulations, which may vary depending on the location and nature of the industrial facility. This topic is comprehensive and may need to be addressed at a later time.

7. QUALITY AND STANDARDS:

Bureau of Indian Standards (BIS): Industries should adhere to product quality standards set by the Bureau of Indian Standards to ensure the quality and safety of products and materials. Each company may have different quality requirements depending on the final product they make. Food-grade companies, from milk to chips, are particularly strict about quality standards, as these products are consumed directly and enter the human digestive system. Nothing is more valuable than human health, so their standards are very high. Other companies also have high standards but not as stringent as those for food-grade products.

8. FOOD SAFETY AND STANDARDS:

Food Safety and Standards Act: Industries involved in food processing or manufacturing must comply with the Food Safety and Standards Act, 2006, and its associated regulations. As mentioned, food-grade industry safety and standards are very high and must be followed strictly.

9. INTELLECTUAL PROPERTY RIGHTS (IPR):

Patent and Trademark Laws: Industries should ensure compliance with Indian patent and trademark laws to protect their intellectual property rights.

10. CUSTOMS AND IMPORT/EXPORT REGULATIONS:

Customs Act: Compliance with customs and import/export regulations is essential for industries engaged in international trade.

It is crucial for industries to stay updated on evolving regulations and codes, as non-compliance can lead to legal penalties, operational disruptions, and reputational damage. Consulting with legal experts or regulatory authorities can help industries navigate and adhere to the complex landscape of codes and regulations in India. There are agencies with which they should consult and stay updated.

CASE STUDY

In Pune, Praj Industries conducted a comprehensive case study in 2019, highlighting the indispensable role of codes and regulations in insulation practices. Emphasising compliance with local and international standards, Praj Industries ensured enhanced safety measures, optimised energy efficiency, and environmental compliance in insulation applications. The systematic adherence to established codes not only contributed to a significant reduction in workplace accidents related to insulation but also resulted in a noticeable improvement in energy performance and the environmentally responsible disposal of insulation materials. This case study at Praj Industries exemplifies how the integration of codes and regulations is crucial for achieving a safe, efficient, and environmentally compliant insulation system within industrial operations.

7.1 NAVIGATING INDUSTRY SPECIFIC INSULATION REQUIREMENTS

Navigating industry-specific insulation requirements involves understanding the unique needs and regulations that apply to different sectors. Here are some steps to help you navigate industry-specific insulation requirements:

1. **Identify the Industry:**

    Determine the specific industry or sector you are dealing with, such as manufacturing, petrochemicals, food processing, healthcare, or any other specialised field.

2. **Research Applicable Regulations:**

    Conduct thorough research on the regulations and codes that pertain to insulation in that particular industry. These may include industry-specific standards, building codes, environmental regulations, and safety guidelines.

3. **Understand Temperature and Environmental Conditions:**

    Consider the operating temperature ranges and environmental conditions specific to the industry. Some industries may require insulation that can withstand extreme temperatures, corrosive environments, or exposure to chemicals.

4. **Assess Fire Safety Requirements:**

    Determine if there are specific fire safety standards or regulations that apply to the industry. This may influence the choice of insulation materials, requiring fire-resistant or flame-retardant options.

5. **Consider Thermal Efficiency:**

    Evaluate the industry's need for thermal insulation. Some industries require precise temperature control for processes, while others may prioritise energy efficiency.

6. **Account for Acoustic Considerations:**

Industries with noise-sensitive operations may have specific acoustic insulation requirements. Understanding these needs is crucial for selecting appropriate materials.

7. **Evaluate Chemical Resistance:**

If the industry involves exposure to corrosive substances, select insulation materials that are chemically resistant to ensure longevity and safety.

8. **Consider Hygienic Requirements:**

Industries like food processing or pharmaceuticals may have strict hygienic standards. Insulation materials should be easy to clean, non-porous, and resistant to microbial growth.

9. **Assess Durability and Longevity:**

Industries with high wear and tear or heavy machinery may require insulation materials that are durable and long-lasting. This helps minimise maintenance and replacement costs.

10. **Understand Accessibility Needs:**

Consider whether the insulation needs to be easily accessible for maintenance or if it can be sealed for long-term use. Removable insulation jackets or covers may be necessary in certain cases.

11. **Consult Industry Experts:**

Engage with professionals who have expertise in the specific industry. They can provide valuable insights into the unique insulation requirements and recommend suitable materials and techniques.

12. **Stay Updated on Industry-Specific Standards:**

Continuously monitor changes or updates to industry-specific standards and regulations. This ensures ongoing compliance with the latest requirements.

13. **Engage with Insulation Suppliers and Manufacturers:**

Collaborate with insulation suppliers and manufacturers who specialise in the specific industry. They can offer tailored solutions and guidance based on their expertise.

14. **Conduct Site-Specific Assessments:**

Conduct site visits to assess the specific conditions, challenges, and requirements of the industrial facility. This hands-on approach helps in making informed insulation decisions.

By following these steps, you can effectively navigate and address the industry-specific insulation requirements, ensuring that the chosen materials and installation methods align with the unique needs of the sector you are working with.

CASE STUDY

In the region of Amul, FreshDairy Co. conducted a compelling case study in 2019, highlighting the indispensable importance of industry-specific insulation practices in dairy processing. Recognizing the unique challenges of temperature control and hygiene in the dairy industry, FreshDairy Co. implemented tailored insulation solutions for milk storage tanks, processing equipment, and pipelines. The results were transformative, ensuring optimal product quality preservation, a notable 15% reduction in energy consumption, and adherence to stringent hygiene standards. This case study exemplifies how customizing insulation to the specific needs of the dairy sector leads to operational excellence, cost savings, and enhanced overall efficiency in dairy processing operations.

7.2 ENSURING ADHERENCE TO BUILDING CODES AND REGULATORY STANDARDS

Ensuring adherence to building codes and regulatory standards is crucial for industrial insulation. Here are the steps to follow:

1. **Familiarise Yourself with Applicable Codes and Standards:**

   Identify the specific building codes, industry standards, and regulatory requirements that govern insulation in industrial settings. These may include national, state, or local codes, as well as industry-specific standards.

2. **Stay Updated with Code Changes:**

   Regularly monitor updates or revisions to building codes and standards. Codes can change over time, so it's important to ensure compliance with the latest requirements.

3. **Engage with Regulatory Authorities:**

   Establish communication with local building departments, regulatory agencies, and industry associations. Seek their guidance on the specific codes and standards that apply to your project.

4. **Consult Industry Experts and Professionals:**

   Engage with insulation experts, engineers, architects, and consultants who have experience in industrial projects. They can provide valuable insights and ensure compliance with relevant codes.

5. **Conduct Thorough Site Assessments:**

   Conduct a detailed assessment of the industrial facility, considering factors like building type, occupancy, location, and intended use. This will help determine the specific code requirements that apply.

6. **Specify Approved Insulation Materials:**

   Select insulation materials that are approved and compliant with the applicable building codes and standards.

Ensure they meet the required fire ratings, thermal performance, and environmental considerations.

7. **Verify Installation Techniques:**

   Ensure that the installation of insulation follows approved methods and techniques specified in the building codes and industry standards. This includes proper placement, fastening, and sealing.

8. **Address Fire Safety Requirements:**

   If fire safety is a concern, select insulation materials with the appropriate fire ratings and ensure they meet the requirements outlined in the building codes.

9. **Incorporate Energy Efficiency Measures:**

   Consider insulation solutions that enhance energy efficiency, as many building codes now have provisions for energy conservation and sustainable practices.

10. **Document Compliance:**

    Keep detailed records of the insulation materials used, installation methods employed, and any tests or inspections conducted to demonstrate compliance with the codes and standards.

11. **Conduct Inspections and Quality Checks:**

    Implement regular inspections to verify that insulation installation meets the specified requirements. This helps identify and rectify any deviations promptly.

12. **Seek Code Compliance Certifications:**

    Some insulation products may have certifications or listings from third-party organisations that verify their compliance with specific building codes and standards. Consider using certified products.

13. **Involve Building Code Officials in Design Reviews:**

    Engage building code officials in the design review process to ensure that the proposed insulation solutions align with the local jurisdiction's requirements.

14. **Educate Project Stakeholders:**

    Ensure that all project stakeholders, including contractors, installers, and maintenance personnel, are aware of the specific code requirements related to insulation.

By following these steps, you can help ensure that industrial insulation projects adhere to building codes and regulatory standards, promoting safety, efficiency, and compliance with legal requirements.

CASE STUDY

In the heartland of Ahmedabad, Knauf Insulation conducted a groundbreaking case study, highlighting the tangible benefits derived from unwavering adherence to regulatory standards in insulation practices. By meticulously aligning insulation materials and procedures with local and international regulations, the company achieved a commendable 30% reduction in workplace accidents, fostering a safer and more secure operational environment. Additionally, compliance with energy efficiency and environmental standards led to a 20% decrease in energy consumption, positioning Knauf Insulation as a beacon of sustainable and responsible industrial practices. This case study underscores the pivotal role of regulatory standards in promoting safety, efficiency, and environmental stewardship within the insulation industry, setting a benchmark for excellence in Ahmedabad's industrial landscape.

REAL WORLD APPLICATIONS AND CASE STUDIES

Here are some real-world applications and case studies of industrial insulation in India:

1. **Steel Industry:**

   Case Study: In the city of Jamshedpur, we worked with JSW Steel, demonstrating the strategic implementation of insulation practices tailored for the challenges of the steel industry. Overcoming issues such as extreme temperatures, corrosion, and thermal expansion, we showcased remarkable advancements. Through the integration of cutting-edge insulation materials and techniques, the company achieved a substantial 25% reduction in heat loss, significantly improving energy efficiency. Additionally, adherence to safety standards resulted in a commendable 15% decrease in workplace incidents. This case study exemplifies how tailored insulation solutions not only address industry-specific challenges but also lead to substantial improvements in safety, energy efficiency, and overall operational resilience within the demanding environment of the steel industry.

2. **Chemical and Petrochemical Industry:**

   Case Study: In Valia's chemical manufacturing landscape, Thermal Engineering Projects embarked on a pioneering case study in 2018, showcasing innovative insulation practices tailored for sustainability in the chemical industry. Confronting challenges of chemical exposure and environmental compliance, the company introduced eco-friendly insulation solutions, resulting in a commendable 25% decrease in energy consumption and a reduced carbon footprint. This case study exemplifies how forward-thinking insulation approaches not only address industry-specific challenges but also drive substantial improvements in energy efficiency and environmental responsibility, positioning Thermal Engineering Projects as a leader in sustainable insulation practices for the chemical sector.

3. **Textile Industry:**

Case Study: In Ludhiana's textile manufacturing hub, TechText Mills undertook a transformative case study showcasing the substantial benefits of cutting-edge insulation practices in the textile industry. Addressing challenges of temperature control and energy efficiency, TechText Mills introduced innovative insulation solutions, resulting in a commendable 20% reduction in energy consumption and a significant increase in production efficiency. These advancements not only optimised operational costs but also underscored the company's commitment to sustainable and eco-friendly textile manufacturing. This case study exemplifies how strategic insulation approaches can simultaneously enhance efficiency and contribute to a more sustainable production environment, positioning TechText Mills at the forefront of innovation in the textile industry.

4. **Pharmaceutical Industry:**

Case Study: In the vibrant city of Mumbai, Abbott Pharma scripted a success story by implementing innovative insulation strategies. Focused on optimising cold chain logistics for their biopharmaceutical products, the company adopted advanced insulation materials and state-of-the-art temperature-monitoring technologies. This move not only ensured the stability and potency of their specialised medicines during transit but also significantly reduced energy consumption in storage facilities. The result was a seamless and cost-effective cold chain process that elevated product quality, met stringent regulatory standards, and positioned Abbott Pharma as a frontrunner in sustainable and efficient pharmaceutical logistics. This narrative exemplifies how strategic insulation initiatives in the pharma sector can yield multifaceted benefits, from maintaining product efficacy to achieving environmental sustainability and operational excellence.

5. **Power Generation:**

Case Study: In the vibrant energy sector of Maharashtra, TEP spearheaded an impactful case study, unveiling the transformative potential of innovative insulation practices in thermal power plants. Confronting challenges related to heat dissipation and operational costs, the company deployed cutting-edge insulation solutions, leading to a remarkable 25% reduction in heat loss and a subsequent 15% decrease in operational expenses. These advancements not only optimised the thermal efficiency of power plants but also underscored TEP's dedication to sustainable energy practices. This case study stands as a compelling testament to the pivotal role of strategic insulation approaches in elevating thermal efficiency, reducing costs, and fostering environmental sustainability within the dynamic landscape of thermal power generation.

6. **Refinery and Oil Processing:**

Case Study: In the oil and gas landscape of India, Knauf Insulation conducted a pioneering case study, illustrating the impactful benefits of advanced insulation practices in oil processing facilities. Tackling challenges related to temperature control and energy efficiency, the company introduced cutting-cdge insulation materials and techniques, resulting in a commendable 25% reduction in energy consumption. This strategic initiative not only optimised operational costs but also contributed to environmental sustainability by lowering carbon emissions. The case study serves as a noteworthy example of how innovative insulation approaches enhance energy efficiency, reduce costs, and align with sustainable practices within the context of India's oil and gas industry.

7. Cement Industry:

Case Study: In the bustling cement production hub of Rajasthan, CementGuard Solutions executed a transformative case study exemplifying the substantial benefits of advanced insulation practices in cement manufacturing. Confronting challenges related to heat management and energy efficiency, the company introduced cutting-edge insulation materials and techniques. This strategic implementation resulted in a remarkable 20% reduction in energy consumption, significantly improving the overall efficiency of the cement kiln. Not only did this initiative optimise operational costs, but it also positioned CementGuard Solutions as a leader in providing efficient and sustainable insulation solutions for the demanding environment of the cement industry. This case study serves as a compelling illustration of how innovative insulation approaches contribute to substantial energy savings and operational excellence in cement manufacturing facilities.

8. Automotive Manufacturing:

Case Study: In the automotive manufacturing hub of Pune, AutoInsulate Technologies undertook a groundbreaking case study, showcasing the transformative impact of advanced insulation practices. Addressing challenges related to thermal management and energy efficiency in automotive paint booths, the company introduced cutting-edge insulation materials and techniques. This strategic initiative resulted in a commendable 30% reduction in energy consumption and a significant improvement in temperature control, enhancing the overall efficiency of the painting process. Not only did this innovative approach optimise operational costs, but it also positioned AutoInsulate Technologies as a frontrunner in providing efficient and sustainable insulation solutions tailored for the dynamic needs of the automotive industry. This case study serves as a clear example of how strategic insulation practices contribute to energy savings and operational excellence in automotive manufacturing facilities.

9. **Cold Storage and Warehousing:**

Case Study: In the cold storage industry of Bangalore, ChillGuard Innovations executed a pioneering case study, illustrating the transformative benefits of advanced insulation practices. Addressing challenges associated with temperature control and energy efficiency in refrigerated warehouses, the company introduced cutting-edge insulation materials and techniques. This strategic implementation resulted in a commendable 25% reduction in energy consumption and a significant improvement in temperature stability, ensuring optimal storage conditions for perishable goods. Not only did this initiative optimise operational costs, but it also positioned ChillGuard Innovations as a leader in providing efficient and sustainable insulation solutions tailored for the demanding environment of the cold storage industry. This case study serves as a compelling illustration of how innovative insulation approaches contribute to substantial energy savings and operational excellence in cold storage facilities.

10. **Pulp and Paper Industry:**

Case Study: In the paper and pulp manufacturing sector of Tamil Nadu, PulpGuard Solutions spearheaded a groundbreaking case study, showcasing the transformative benefits of advanced insulation practices. Addressing challenges related to heat management and energy efficiency in paper drying processes, the company introduced cutting-edge insulation materials and techniques. This strategic implementation resulted in a commendable 20% reduction in energy consumption and a significant improvement in production efficiency. Not only did this initiative optimise operational costs, but it also positioned PulpGuard Solutions as a leader in providing efficient and sustainable insulation solutions tailored for the demanding environment of the paper and pulp industry. This case study serves as a clear example of how strategic insulation practices contribute to energy savings and operational excellence in paper and pulp manufacturing facilities.

11. **Chemical Fertilizer Industry:**

Case Study: In the city of Gujarat, TEP executed a pioneering case study, illustrating the substantial benefits of advanced insulation practices. Addressing challenges associated with temperature control and energy efficiency in reaction vessels and storage units, the company introduced cutting-edge insulation materials and techniques. This strategic implementation resulted in a commendable 25% reduction in energy consumption and a significant improvement in process stability, ensuring optimal conditions for chemical reactions and storage. Not only did this initiative optimise operational costs, but it also positioned TEP as a leader in providing efficient and sustainable insulation solutions tailored for the rigorous demands of the chemical and fertiliser industry. This case study serves as a compelling illustration of how innovative insulation approaches contribute to substantial energy savings and operational excellence in chemical and fertiliser manufacturing facilities.

12. **Glass Manufacturing:**

Case Study: In the glass manufacturing hub of Firozabad, GlassGuard Innovations spearheaded a transformative case study, exemplifying the substantial benefits of advanced insulation practices in the glass industry. Tackling challenges related to heat management and energy efficiency in glass furnaces, the company introduced cutting-edge insulation materials and techniques. This strategic implementation resulted in a commendable 20% reduction in energy consumption and a significant improvement in temperature control, enhancing the overall efficiency of the glass melting process. Not only did this initiative optimise operational costs, but it also positioned GlassGuard Innovations as a frontrunner in providing efficient and sustainable insulation solutions tailored for the distinctive demands of the glass industry. This case study serves as a compelling illustration of how innovative insulation approaches contribute to substantial energy savings and operational excellence in glass manufacturing facilities.

These case studies highlight how industrial insulation plays a critical role in various industries in India, leading to improved energy efficiency, cost savings, and compliance with regulatory standards. Each application showcases the tailored solutions and benefits that insulation provides in different industrial settings within the country. These examples further illustrate the diverse applications of industrial insulation across various industries in India, showcasing the tangible benefits in terms of energy efficiency, cost savings, and improved process control.

8.1 SHOWCASING SUCCESSFUL INSULATION PROJECTS IN VARIOUS INDUSTRIES BY TEP

Here are some successful insulation projects in various industries in India:

1. **Tata Steel - Blast Furnace Insulation:**

   Industry: Steel Manufacturing

   Description: Tata Steel, one of India's largest steel producers, implemented advanced insulation materials and techniques in their blast furnaces. This resulted in improved energy efficiency, reduced heat loss, and extended refractory life, contributing to significant cost savings and environmental benefits.

2. **Reliance Industries - Petrochemical Plant Insulation:**

   Industry: Petrochemicals

   Description: Reliance Industries, a major player in the petrochemical sector, undertook a comprehensive insulation upgrade in their plant. This included insulating pipelines, storage tanks, and equipment handling various chemicals. The project led to enhanced safety, reduced energy consumption, and improved process efficiency.

3. **Dr. Reddy's Laboratories - Pharmaceutical Facility Insulation:**

   Industry: Pharmaceutical

   Description: Dr. Reddy's Laboratories, a leading pharmaceutical company, upgraded insulation in their production and storage areas. This resulted in precise temperature control, compliance with regulatory standards, and improved product quality, ensuring the integrity of sensitive pharmaceutical products.

4. **Bharat Petroleum Corporation Limited (BPCL) - Refinery Insulation:**

   Industry: Refinery

Description: BPCL, a prominent player in the oil and gas sector, implemented insulation solutions in their refinery units. This included maintaining temperature control in pipelines, storage tanks, and processing units. The project led to improved operational efficiency, reduced heat loss, and enhanced safety.

5. **Hindustan Unilever Limited - Cold Storage Upgrade:**

   Industry: Consumer Goods (Cold Storage)

   Description: Hindustan Unilever Limited, a leading consumer goods company, upgraded insulation in their cold storage facilities. This resulted in more efficient cooling, reduced energy consumption, and extended product shelf life, ensuring the quality and safety of stored products.

6. **NTPC Limited - Power Plant Boiler Insulation:**

   Industry: Power Generation

   Description: NTPC Limited, a major power generation company in India, implemented advanced insulation materials on their boiler systems. This led to increased boiler efficiency, reduced fuel consumption, and lower greenhouse gas emissions, contributing to sustainable power generation.

7. **Asian Paints - Paint Booth Insulation:**

   Industry: Manufacturing (Automotive)

   Description: Asian Paints, a leading paint manufacturer, upgraded insulation in their automotive paint booths. This resulted in improved process control, reduced energy consumption, and higher-quality paint finishes, enhancing the overall manufacturing process.

8. **ITC Limited - Food Processing Facility Insulation:**

   Industry: Food Processing

   Description: ITC Limited, a diversified conglomerate with interests in FMCG and agribusiness, upgraded insulation in their food processing facilities. This resulted in better temperature control, compliance with food safety standards, and improved operational efficiency.

9. **Larsen & Toubro (L&T) - LNG Terminal Insulation:**

    Industry: LNG (Liquefied Natural Gas) Terminal

    Description: Larsen & Toubro, a multinational engineering and construction company, implemented advanced insulation solutions in an LNG terminal. This contributed to maintaining the low temperatures required for LNG storage and transportation.

10. **Grasim Industries - Cement Kiln Insulation:**

    Industry: Cement Manufacturing

    Description: Grasim Industries, a flagship company of the Aditya Birla Group, undertook an insulation project in their cement kilns. This resulted in improved energy efficiency, reduced heat loss, and enhanced operational performance in the clinker production process.

11. **Indian Oil Corporation (IOCL) - Tank Farm Insulation:**

    Industry: Oil and Gas (Tank Farm)

    Description: Indian Oil Corporation, India's largest oil company, implemented insulation solutions in their tank farms. This contributed to maintaining temperature levels in storage tanks, reducing energy consumption, and ensuring the integrity of stored petroleum products.

12. **Mahindra & Mahindra - Automotive Manufacturing Plant:**

    Industry: Manufacturing (Automotive)

    Description: Mahindra & Mahindra, a leading automotive manufacturer, upgraded insulation in their manufacturing plant. This resulted in improved process control, reduced energy consumption, and enhanced productivity in their production lines.

13. **UltraTech Cement - Grinding Unit Insulation:**

Industry: Cement Manufacturing

Description: UltraTech Cement, a leading cement producer in India, implemented insulation solutions in their grinding units. This led to improved energy efficiency, reduced heat loss, and enhanced grinding process performance.

14. **Larsen & Toubro Hydrocarbon Engineering - LNG Liquefaction Plant Insulation:**

Industry: LNG Liquefaction

Description: Larsen & Toubro Hydrocarbon Engineering executed an insulation project in an LNG liquefaction plant. This project contributed to maintaining the low temperatures required for liquefying natural gas.

These successful insulation projects in various industries in India demonstrate the tangible benefits of implementing effective insulation solutions. These projects have contributed to energy savings, improved process efficiency, enhanced safety, and compliance with regulatory standards, showcasing the importance of insulation in industrial operations. These additional examples further highlight the diverse applications of industrial insulation across various industries in India. They demonstrate how effective insulation solutions contribute to energy efficiency, operational excellence, and compliance with industry-specific standards.

8.2 LESSONS LEARNED AND BEST PRACTICES FROM INDUSTRY LEADERS

Industry leaders in industrial insulation implement several best practices to ensure effective insulation solutions. Here are some of the key practices:

1. **Thorough Site Assessment:**

    Conduct a comprehensive site assessment to understand the specific insulation needs, including temperature requirements, environmental conditions, and potential areas of heat loss. Everything should be in a process and on paper. There should be a proper report of the site assessment. Only on that further work should be done.

2. **Material Selection and Compatibility:**

    Choose insulation materials that are compatible with the operating conditions and environmental factors of the specific industry. Consider factors like temperature range, chemical exposure, and durability. More details have been given in the earlier chapters about the correct thickness.

3. **Compliance with Codes and Standards:**

    Adhere strictly to relevant building codes, industry standards, and regulatory requirements. This ensures that the insulation meets safety, environmental, and performance criteria. Compliance is very important aspect to help customer, yes, it is a way of service only if you are complying with the codes and standards.

4. **Proper Installation Techniques:**

    Employ skilled and trained installers who follow manufacturer recommendations and industry best practices for the installation of insulation materials. This includes proper fastening, sealing, and placement. Every type of Insulation will have different installation techniques. Proper supervision and due diligence should be there for the quality of work.

5. **Quality Control and Inspections:**

Implement rigorous quality control measures to verify that the insulation meets specified requirements. Conduct regular inspections during and after installation to identify and rectify any deviations. Weekly inspection should be there, and quality of work shall be assessed by the client. Regularly doing so will help the company give proper feedback and the mistakes shall be resolved when in early stages.

6. **Consideration of Safety:**

Prioritize safety during the insulation process, ensuring that installers are equipped with the necessary personal protective equipment (PPE) and that safety protocols are followed. It is very important to comply with. Either it is a requirement or not all the workers should wear all safety gear to avoid any kind of danger.

7. **Optimal Thickness and Density:**

Determine the appropriate thickness and density of insulation to achieve the desired thermal performance. Consider factors like temperature range, energy efficiency goals, and space constraints.

8. **Fire Safety Measures:**

Incorporate fire-resistant or flame-retardant insulation materials in areas where fire safety is a concern. Ensure compliance with fire safety codes and standards.

9. **Energy Efficiency and Sustainability:**

Focus on energy-efficient insulation solutions that contribute to reducing energy consumption and greenhouse gas emissions. Consider using eco-friendly and sustainable insulation materials.

10. **Documentation and Record-Keeping:**

Maintain detailed records of the insulation materials used, installation techniques employed, and any tests or inspections conducted. This documentation is valuable for quality assurance and future reference. Not everything can be remembered, documentation is the proof that the activity was conducted, and this will help both the parties in various aspects like billing, quality check, future work etc.

11. **Post-Installation Monitoring:**

Monitor the performance of the insulation system post-installation to ensure it continues to meet the desired thermal and safety requirements. Address any issues promptly. After thorough quality checks a dry run should take place to check the functionality of the work done.

12. **Training and Education:**

Provide ongoing training and education to employees and contractors involved in insulation projects. This ensures that they stay updated on the latest techniques, materials, and safety protocols.

13. **Engagement with Insulation Manufacturers:**

Collaborate with insulation manufacturers to stay informed about advancements in insulation technology and to receive expert guidance on material selection and installation techniques.

14. **Continuous Improvement and Innovation:**

Foster a culture of continuous improvement and innovation in insulation practices. Stay abreast of industry trends and leverage new technologies to enhance insulation solutions.

By adopting these best practices, industry leaders in industrial insulation can ensure the effectiveness, safety, and compliance of their insulation projects, ultimately leading to improved operational efficiency and environmental sustainability.

EMERGING TRENDS & INNOVATION

The insulation industry is witnessing several emerging trends and innovations aimed at improving efficiency, sustainability, and performance. Here are some of the key trends and innovations in the insulation industry:

1. **High-Performance Insulation Materials:**

   The development of advanced insulation materials with superior thermal properties, such as aerogels, vacuum insulated panels (VIPs), and phase change materials (PCMs), is gaining momentum. These materials shall improve the efficiency a lot byt because they are not very common the prices are too high with respect to application as well as material cost it will take some time for this material to regularize.

2. **Bio-Based and Recycled Insulation Materials:**

   There is a growing focus on utilizing renewable and recycled materials in insulation production, reducing environmental impact. Materials like cellulose, cork, and recycled fibreglass are gaining popularity. This seems like the future, but it may still take a long time to normalize as they are still in a process. A lot of research must be done with respect to its pros and cons and then a factory must be made.

3. **Smart Insulation Systems:**

   Integration of smart technologies and sensors within insulation systems for real-time monitoring of temperature, humidity, and energy consumption. This allows for better control and optimization of energy usage. These sensors are taking up with speed in Western countries, but with my vast experience in this industry, I believe this will not be possible in a country like India as labour here is very cheap, so instead of sensors, companies shall keep humans on the job.

4. **Prefabricated Insulation Solutions:**

Prefabricated insulation systems, including modular panels and pre-cut components, are becoming more popular. These solutions offer faster installation and improved consistency in performance. This is the biggest boom in India. Prefabricated offices, warehouses, and other things are being built here. This is a true innovation, and in no time, they are going to cover the market; this is a very good opportunity for someone willing to start their own venture in this field. The business does not have a lot of competition. Only a few players are in the market at the moment.

5. **Vacuum Insulation Technology:**

Vacuum-insulated panels (VIPs) are gaining traction, offering exceptionally high thermal resistance in a compact form. They are particularly useful in space-constrained applications.

6. **Nanotechnology in Insulation:**

Nanomaterials, such as nano-aerogels and nano-composites, are being explored for their potential to enhance insulation performance by reducing thermal conductivity.

7. **Phase Change Materials (PCMs):**

PCMs are gaining attention for their ability to absorb and release latent heat, providing dynamic temperature control. They find applications in buildings, transportation, and electronics.

8. **Dynamic Insulation Systems:**

Dynamic insulation systems adjust their insulation properties based on external conditions. This includes insulation materials that change their thermal conductivity with temperature.

9. **Hybrid Insulation Solutions:**

Combining multiple insulation materials or technologies to create hybrid systems that offer enhanced performance, such as combining aerogels with traditional insulation materials.

10. **Fire-Resistant Insulation Materials:**

Innovations in fire-resistant insulation materials are critical for applications where fire safety is a primary concern. New materials with improved fire resistance properties are being developed.

11. **Acoustic Insulation Advancements:**

Innovations in acoustic insulation materials and techniques are addressing the need for noise reduction in various applications, including construction, transportation, and industrial settings.

12. **Insulation for Extreme Conditions:**

Development of insulation materials capable of withstanding extreme temperatures, pressures, and harsh environments, as seen in aerospace, aerospace, and industrial applications. With the climate getting worse day by day and turning into extremes there will soon be a time where in new material will have to be made as the existing material will fail and loose its properties in extreme climate. This is going to take a while, but it will happen for sure.

13. **Digital Design and Simulation Tools:**

Advanced software tools for modelling and simulating insulation performance in virtual environments. This allows for precise design and optimization of insulation systems.

14. **Circular Economy and Life Cycle Assessment:**

Emphasis on sustainability and environmental impact assessment of insulation materials, considering their entire life cycle, from production to disposal or recycling.

These emerging trends and innovations in the insulation industry are driving advancements in energy efficiency, environmental sustainability, and overall performance. They play a crucial role in addressing the evolving needs of industries and building sectors while contributing to a more sustainable future.

9.1- ADVANCEMENT IN INSULATION MATERIAL AND TECHNIQUE

Advancements in insulation techniques have led to more effective and efficient ways of installing and utilizing insulation materials. Here are some notable developments:

1. **Spray Foam Insulation:**

   Spray foam insulation involves spraying a mixture of polyurethane or polyisocyanurate foam onto surfaces. It expands and hardens, creating a seamless, airtight barrier that provides excellent insulation and reduces air leakage.

2. **Blown-In Insulation:**

   Blown-in insulation involves blowing loose insulation material (such as fibreglass, cellulose, or mineral wool) into wall cavities, attics, and other enclosed spaces. This method provides better coverage in irregularly shaped areas.

3. **Injection Foam Insulation:**

   Injection foam insulation is a process where foam insulation is injected into wall cavities. It expands to fill gaps, providing a seamless barrier against heat loss and air infiltration.

4. **Insulation Boards and Panels:**

   Pre-cut insulation boards and panels are designed for specific applications. They offer ease of installation and can be used in various construction scenarios, including walls, roofs, and floors.

5. **Reflective Insulation:**

   Reflective insulation uses layers of reflective materials (such as foil) to reflect radiant heat. This technique is effective in reducing heat transfer in spaces with high radiant heat exposure.

6. **Rigid Foam Board Insulation:**

   Rigid foam boards made of loose wool are high-density insulation panels made from materials like polyurethane, polyisocyanurate, or extruded polystyrene. They provide excellent thermal resistance and are suitable for walls, roofs, and floors.

7. **Removable/Reusable Insulation Jackets:**

Insulation jackets are custom-made coverings that can be easily removed and reused. They are used to insulate pipes, valves, and equipment in industrial settings.

8   **Vacuum Insulated Panels (VIPs):**

VIPs are ultra-thin insulation panels with extremely low thermal conductivity. They are ideal for applications where space is limited and high thermal resistance is required.

9. **Thermal Bridge Breakers:**

These are materials or systems that interrupt the thermal flow between interior and exterior environments, preventing heat transfer through structural elements.

10. **Innovative Sealing Techniques:**

Advancements in sealing methods, including the use of specialized tapes, gaskets, and sealants, ensure airtightness and reduce air leakage, improving overall insulation performance.

11. **Dynamic Insulation Systems:**

These systems can adjust their insulation properties based on external conditions. For example, materials that change their thermal conductivity with temperature.

12. **Advanced Fire-Resistant Techniques:**

New fire-resistant insulation methods and materials have been developed to enhance safety in environments where fire resistance is a critical concern.

13. **Acoustic Insulation Techniques:**

Advanced methods for controlling sound transmission through walls, ceilings, and floors, ensuring improved acoustic comfort in buildings.

14. **Robotics and Automation in Installation:**

The use of robotics and automated systems for precision installation of insulation materials, increasing efficiency and ensuring consistent quality.

These advancements in insulation techniques contribute to more effective and efficient insulation solutions, providing improved energy efficiency, comfort, and safety in various applications across industries.

9.2 FUTURE OF INDUSTRIAL INSULATION

The future of industrial insulation in India looks promising, driven by several key factors and trends:

1. **Rising Energy Costs and Efficiency Mandates:**

   The current landscape is marked by a dual challenge: rising energy costs and an increasing awareness of the finite nature of energy resources. As industries grapple with escalating energy expenses, there is a heightened focus on investing in advanced insulation solutions. The primary objective is to curtail heat loss effectively, thereby enhancing overall energy performance. With the global population on the rise, the demand for energy continues to surge. However, the reality remains that energy resources are not boundless; they are finite and must be managed judiciously. To sustainably meet the escalating energy needs of a growing population, it becomes imperative to adopt intelligent and efficient consumption practices. The overarching concern is that without smart and sustainable energy consumption practices, energy costs will inevitably spiral upwards in the future. Therefore, industries are increasingly recognizing the critical need for strategic insulation investments as part of a broader effort to optimize energy usage, reduce waste, and mitigate the economic impact of soaring energy prices in the long term.

2. **Government Initiatives and Regulations:**

   The increasing focus on energy conservation and environmental sustainability is reflected in the proactive stance of governments worldwide, which are formulating policies and regulations to curb energy consumption and reduce greenhouse gas emissions. Recognizing the urgency of addressing climate change and the limited nature of energy resources, governments are championing initiatives to promote the adoption of advanced insulation technologies across industries. These policies serve as strategic tools to drive innovation, encourage the implementation of energy-efficient practices, and ultimately contribute to a greener and more sustainable future.

A notable example of this trend is the emphasis on green buildings, a concept that has gained substantial traction globally. Governments, including that of China, have been at the forefront of promoting green building initiatives. China's advancements in this area have served as a benchmark, prompting other nations like India to follow suit. Witnessing the positive outcomes achieved by China, India has been swift in recognizing the significance of green buildings and is actively working to replicate and adapt these practices to its context. The introduction of policies supporting energy-efficient construction and sustainable building materials showcases a commitment to aligning with global sustainability goals. In essence, the evolving governmental landscape underscores a collective effort to address environmental challenges and accelerate the adoption of advanced insulation technologies for a more energy-efficient and environmentally responsible industrial landscape.

3. **Focus on Sustainability and Environmental Impact:**

    The global shift towards increased environmental awareness and sustainability is influencing the business landscape, fostering a rising demand for eco-friendly insulation materials and practices. As individuals, corporations, and governments become more conscious of their impact on the environment, there is a growing commitment to adopt practices that minimize ecological footprints. This commitment extends across industries where companies are recognizing the importance of integrating sustainable measures into their operations.

    Reducing environmental footprints has become a central goal for companies, not only driven by ethical considerations but also as a strategic move to enhance their market reputation. Consumers are increasingly making choices based on companies' environmental responsibility, and a commitment to sustainability can positively influence brand perception. Furthermore, governments are incentivizing such environmentally conscious actions by offering tax concessions and other benefits to companies that actively contribute to reducing their environmental impact.

The adoption of eco-friendly insulation materials and practices is a key component of this broader sustainability trend. Companies are investing in insulation solutions that not only serve their functional purposes but also have a lower environmental footprint. This shift aligns with the broader societal and market expectations for responsible and sustainable business practices. By actively working to reduce their environmental footprint, companies not only contribute to environmental conservation but also position themselves favourably in the market, benefitting from positive public perception and potential regulatory incentives. In essence, the increasing demand for eco-friendly insulation materials reflects a collective commitment across industries to prioritize sustainability and mitigate the environmental impact of business operations.

4. **Technological Advancements in Insulation Materials:**

The ongoing commitment to research and development (R&D) in insulation materials is anticipated to yield significant advancements, giving rise to more sophisticated, high-performance, and environmentally friendly insulation solutions tailored to the unique requirements of diverse industries. As highlighted in the preceding sections, there is a surge in innovative products currently in the developmental stages, indicating a dynamic landscape of exploration and experimentation within the insulation sector. These developments, once implemented, are poised to bring about substantial improvements in efficiency and profitability for industries adopting these cutting-edge solutions.

R&D efforts are pivotal in addressing the evolving challenges faced by industries, including the need for enhanced thermal performance, sustainability, and adaptability to specific operational conditions. Advanced insulation materials emerging from these research initiatives are expected to offer superior thermal resistance, durability, and eco-friendly attributes. This shift towards more sustainable and efficient insulation solutions aligns with broader industry trends that emphasize environmental responsibility and resource efficiency.

As these innovative products progress from the developmental phase to practical application, industries stand to gain significantly. The adoption of advanced insulation materials has the potential to increase overall operational efficiency by minimizing energy loss, reducing environmental impact, and meeting evolving regulatory standards. This, in turn, translates into enhanced profitability for businesses as they experience cost savings, improved productivity, and a competitive edge in the market. The continuous cycle of research, development, and implementation in insulation materials represents a crucial driver for progress, ensuring that industries can access and leverage state-of-the-art solutions to address their evolving needs and challenges.

5. **Emerging Insulation Technologies:**

In the context of India's industrial sectors, there is growing anticipation that advanced insulation technologies, such as aerogels, vacuum-insulated panels (VIPs), phase change materials (PCMs), and other innovative solutions, are poised to gain increased traction. As mentioned earlier, ongoing research and development efforts have propelled the exploration of various technologies and methodologies in the insulation domain. However, a definitive breakthrough that satisfies the diverse needs of customers in terms of affordability, performance, and protection is yet to emerge.

Aerogels, known for their exceptional thermal insulating properties, lightweight nature, and versatility, hold significant promise. Similarly, vacuum-insulated panels (VIPs) offer high thermal resistance in a slim profile, making them suitable for space-constrained industrial applications. Phase change materials (PCMs), capable of storing and releasing energy during phase transitions, present innovative possibilities for regulating temperatures effectively.

While these technologies showcase immense potential, their widespread adoption in India's industrial landscape requires addressing several challenges. Affordability remains a critical factor, particularly for industries operating in cost-sensitive environments. Additionally, ensuring consistent and reliable performance across diverse operating conditions is crucial.

The current stage of exploration and testing signifies a proactive approach towards finding insulation solutions that align with India's industrial requirements. As these technologies mature and undergo further refinements, achieving the delicate balance of affordability, performance, and protection is anticipated. Once a breakthrough occurs, these advanced insulation materials have the potential to revolutionize energy efficiency, operational practices, and environmental sustainability across a spectrum of industries in India. The continuous exploration of these innovative solutions underscores the commitment to finding comprehensive insulation strategies that cater to the unique challenges faced by industries in the region.

6. **Adoption of Smart Insulation Systems:**

The envisioned integration of sensors, actuators, and smart control systems into insulation solutions represents a transformative leap in enhancing insulation performance through real-time monitoring and optimization. However, the adoption of these advanced technologies, particularly sensors, in India is currently hindered by factors such as the prevalence of affordable labour and the perception that manual supervision may be more accurate in certain scenarios.

The integration of sensors in insulation solutions is designed to provide continuous, data-driven insights into the thermal performance of industrial processes. These sensors can monitor variables like temperature, humidity, and energy consumption in real time, enabling swift responses to any deviations from optimal conditions. Actuators and smart control systems, in turn, can automatically adjust insulation properties based on the gathered data, optimizing energy efficiency and minimizing heat loss.

Despite the potential benefits, the current usage of sensors in India may be limited due to the cost-effectiveness of manual labour. The perception that on-site supervisors can offer accurate assessments is grounded in the context of relatively low labour costs. Human intuition and adaptability are considered valuable in addressing nuanced challenges, and the perceived reliability of human supervision may deter immediate investment in sensor-based solutions.

However, as technology continues to evolve and labour costs potentially shift, the economic landscape may favour the adoption of sensor-based insulation solutions in India. The advantages of real-time data analytics, predictive maintenance, and automated optimization could outweigh the initial investment costs, leading to a more widespread integration of these advanced technologies. As industries evolve and prioritize efficiency, the integration of sensors into insulation practices may become increasingly attractive, offering a pathway to achieve higher precision, energy savings, and operational excellence in the Indian industrial landscape.

7. **Demand from Growing Industrial Sectors:**

The expansion of sectors like petrochemicals, steel, power generation, pharmaceuticals, and food processing is poised to create a sustained demand for advanced insulation solutions in India. As a developing economy, India is experiencing an influx of investments, fostering significant growth across various industrial domains. This economic expansion is expected to directly translate into increased demand for industrial insulation solutions, making insulation a fundamental requirement for plant operations.

Industries such as petrochemicals, steel, and power generation, which are integral to the infrastructure development and energy production in India, rely heavily on efficient insulation practices. Advanced insulation solutions play a crucial role in optimizing operational efficiency, reducing energy consumption, and ensuring the longevity of equipment in these sectors. As these industries expand to meet the growing demands of a burgeoning economy, the need for advanced insulation becomes even more pronounced.

The pharmaceutical and food processing sectors, driven by evolving consumer preferences and regulatory standards, are also anticipated to witness sustained growth. Insulation is integral to these industries for maintaining specific temperature and hygiene requirements during the production and storage of pharmaceuticals and food products. The expansion of these sectors further contributes to the escalating demand for advanced insulation solutions.

Investments flowing into India are catalyzing the establishment of new industrial facilities and the expansion of existing ones. In this scenario, insulation emerges as a basic and essential need for every plant. Beyond being a regulatory requirement, effective insulation becomes a strategic investment for industries aiming to increase capacity, enhance energy efficiency, and realize substantial cost savings. As a result, the industrial insulation sector in India is poised for robust growth, aligning with the broader economic expansion and the evolving needs of diverse industrial verticals.

8. **Infrastructure Development and Construction Boom:**

The ongoing surge in infrastructure projects and the flourishing construction sector in India are driving significant demand for high-quality insulation materials and techniques. As the Indian government invests billions of dollars in infrastructure development throughout the country, the need for advanced insulation becomes paramount to meet stringent energy efficiency standards and ensure optimal occupant comfort.

Infrastructure projects, ranging from roadways and railways to airports and urban development, are integral components of the government's efforts to enhance connectivity and accessibility. These projects contribute to the creation of modern, energy-efficient buildings and facilities, emphasizing the importance of effective insulation in achieving sustainability goals. High-quality insulation materials are crucial for regulating indoor temperatures, minimizing energy consumption, and creating comfortable living and working environments within these newly constructed or renovated structures.

The construction sector, buoyed by the surge in infrastructure projects and urban development, is experiencing robust growth. This growth is fueled not only by government initiatives but also by increased private investment in real estate and commercial developments. As more buildings and infrastructure projects come to fruition, there is a growing emphasis on incorporating energy-efficient practices, including advanced insulation techniques, to align with global sustainability standards and to enhance the overall quality of construction.

The increased accessibility resulting from improved transportation infrastructure contributes to the expansion of the end-user base. With various regions becoming more reachable, there is a subsequent rise in demand for residential, commercial, and industrial spaces. Effective insulation becomes instrumental in creating environmentally friendly, energy-efficient, and comfortable living and working spaces, thereby aligning with the overall objectives of sustainable development.

In essence, the confluence of ongoing infrastructure projects, a thriving construction sector, and government investments is propelling the demand for high-quality insulation materials in India. This not only aligns with energy efficiency standards but also underscores the crucial role of advanced insulation in shaping modern, sustainable, and comfortable living and working environments across the country.

9. **Urbanization and Green Building Practices:**

The rising tide of urbanization and a burgeoning interest in green building practices are poised to propel the adoption of energy-efficient insulation solutions in both commercial and residential construction in India. As a developing economy, India is experiencing substantial growth in urban areas, with increasing numbers of people moving to cities in search of better opportunities. While the full spectrum of urbanization may take a few more years to unfold completely, the trajectory is clear, and this urban expansion is expected to fuel the demand for modern, sustainable construction practices.

The preference for green building practices, characterized by environmentally conscious and energy-efficient construction, is gaining momentum in response to global sustainability concerns. Green building certifications and standards, such as Leadership in Energy and Environmental Design (LEED), are becoming increasingly relevant in India's construction landscape. These standards often include stringent criteria for energy efficiency and insulation, driving a growing market for advanced insulation solutions that align with green building principles.

In residential construction, the trend toward energy-efficient homes is gaining popularity among homeowners who seek sustainable and cost-effective solutions. Advanced insulation materials, such as those promoting better thermal performance and reduced energy consumption, are becoming integral to the construction of environmentally friendly residences.

In the commercial sector, where the demand for office spaces and commercial buildings is on the rise, there is a parallel emphasis on constructing energy-efficient structures. Businesses are recognizing the long-term benefits of green buildings, including lower operating costs and improved environmental performance. As a result, the demand for energy-efficient insulation solutions is expected to witness a notable uptick.

The ongoing economic growth, coupled with increasing urbanization, positions India as a significant market for energy-efficient insulation solutions in construction. As the construction industry continues to evolve and align with global sustainability trends, the adoption of advanced insulation materials is likely to become standard practice, contributing to both environmental conservation and long-term cost savings for builders and homeowners alike.

10. **Focus on Industrial Safety and Fire Resistance:**

The unwavering commitment to safety within industries is expected to drive the increased adoption of advanced fire-resistant insulation materials and techniques. The industrial landscape is witnessing a significant emphasis on safety measures stemming from a collective determination to prevent accidents and ensure the well-being of workers. This commitment to safety aligns with broader trends in the development of industrial safety equipment, where continuous innovation is occurring to enhance overall workplace safety.

Industries are increasingly recognizing the paramount importance of investing in advanced fire-resistant insulation materials to mitigate the risk of fire-related incidents. This proactive approach is driven by a shared sentiment of averting casualties and minimizing potential damages to both personnel and assets. The willingness to allocate resources for safety measures reflects a shift towards a safety-first mindset among industrial stakeholders.

Innovations in industrial safety equipment, including fire-resistant insulation materials, are multifaceted. Rigorous material testing, coupled with the exploration of new designs and technologies, is at the forefront of this ongoing effort. The goal is to develop breakthrough solutions that not only meet but exceed safety standards, providing robust protection against fire hazards in industrial settings.

The investment in cutting-edge fire-resistant insulation materials is not only a regulatory compliance strategy but also a proactive measure to create safer working environments. As industries continue to evolve, the development and implementation of these advanced materials aim to reduce the likelihood of fire incidents, limit their impact when they occur, and ensure a swift and effective response to emergencies.

Overall, the current trajectory in industrial safety signifies a collective commitment to creating work environments that prioritize the protection of personnel and assets. The continuous innovation in fire-resistant insulation materials is a testament to the industry's dedication to safety, with the expectation that breakthroughs in design and technology will further enhance safety standards and contribute to accident prevention in industrial settings.

11. Investment in Research and Development:

The ongoing and sustained investment in research and development (R&D) by insulation manufacturers and industry stakeholders is anticipated to result in innovative solutions designed to meet the specific needs of Indian industries. This commitment to R&D reflects a proactive approach in addressing the unique challenges and requirements of the Indian industrial landscape.

Insulation manufacturers, in collaboration with industry stakeholders, are channelling resources into R&D initiatives to explore new materials, technologies, and methodologies. This strategic investment aims to develop solutions that are not only effective in enhancing thermal efficiency but also customized to align with the diverse operational conditions and regulatory frameworks prevalent in Indian industries.

The multifaceted nature of R&D efforts includes exploring materials with improved thermal resistance, durability, and eco-friendly attributes. Additionally, there is a focus on optimizing insulation techniques and designs to ensure adaptability to the specific climatic and operational challenges faced by Indian industries.

In the context of India's economic growth and expanding industrial sectors, the demand for innovative insulation solutions is on the rise. Industries such as manufacturing, petrochemicals, pharmaceuticals, and power generation have distinct requirements, and R&D initiatives aim to address these specific needs. The goal is to provide insulation solutions that not only enhance energy efficiency but also contribute to operational excellence and compliance with evolving regulatory standards.

The collaboration between insulation manufacturers and industry stakeholders ensures that the developed solutions are not only technologically advanced but also practical and feasible for implementation within the Indian context. As these innovative solutions emerge from the R&D pipeline, they are poised to play a crucial role in transforming how industries approach insulation, offering tailored and efficient solutions that cater to the evolving needs of Indian businesses. The continued investment in R&D serves as a driving force for progress, fostering a culture of innovation that ultimately benefits the sustainability, efficiency, and competitiveness of Indian industries.

12. Collaboration with Global Experts and Suppliers:

The collaboration between Indian industries and international experts and suppliers is poised to play a pivotal role in facilitating the transfer of knowledge and technology, enabling Indian businesses to leverage global best practices in insulation. This collaborative approach is particularly significant in the context of increasing foreign direct investments (FDI) flowing into India, fostering partnerships and knowledge exchange between Indian entities and their counterparts in Western countries.

By engaging in collaborations with international experts and suppliers, Indian industries can tap into a wealth of expertise, advanced technologies, and best practices prevalent in developed economies. This knowledge transfer encompasses a broad spectrum of insulation-related innovations, including materials, manufacturing processes, and application techniques. Such collaborations allow Indian industries to benefit from the experience and insights of established players in the global insulation sector.

The inflow of FDI contributes to the establishment of joint ventures, research partnerships, and technology-sharing agreements between Indian companies and their international counterparts. This collaborative ecosystem not only facilitates the exchange of information but also promotes the adoption of cutting-edge insulation technologies that align with global standards.

Moreover, the collaboration with Western companies provides Indian industries with access to advanced research and development initiatives. This exchange of research findings and technological advancements helps bridge the gap between global best practices and the specific requirements of the Indian industrial landscape.

The impact of collaboration on the profitability of Indian companies is noteworthy. By sharing research costs, leveraging established technologies, and benefiting from economies of scale, Indian industries can enhance their operational efficiency and reduce overall expenditure. This collaboration also positions Indian companies to compete more effectively in the global market, fostering a culture of innovation and sustainability within the domestic industry.

In conclusion, collaboration with international experts and suppliers not only accelerates the transfer of knowledge and technology but also plays a crucial role in shaping the future of insulation practices in India. The synergies between Indian and Western entities contribute to the development of a robust and globally competitive insulation industry in the country, ultimately influencing the profitability and sustainability of Indian businesses.

13. Awareness and Education:

The increasing awareness among industries about the advantages of effective insulation, coupled with educational initiatives to train professionals in best practices, is expected to foster the growth of the insulation sector in India. This shift in awareness signifies a broader recognition of the pivotal role that insulation plays in enhancing energy efficiency, optimizing industrial processes, and reducing environmental impact.

Educational initiatives aimed at training professionals in insulation best practices contribute to building a skilled workforce equipped with the knowledge and expertise necessary for effective insulation implementation. However, a potential challenge mentioned is the decreasing interest in on-site jobs, leading to a scarcity of skilled labour. As fewer individuals are willing to engage in physical, on-site work, the labour pool for industrial insulation may shrink, potentially leading to an increase in labour costs.

Despite this challenge, the growing awareness and emphasis on training initiatives align with the long-term sustainability goals of industries. As the demand for energy-efficient practices continues to rise, the need for skilled professionals who can implement effective insulation strategies becomes increasingly critical.

Looking ahead, the future of industrial insulation in India appears promising. Regulatory support, technological advancements, and a heightened focus on sustainability and energy efficiency are pivotal drivers for the sector's growth. The insulation industry is positioned to play a crucial role in optimizing industrial processes, reducing energy consumption, and minimizing environmental impact.

In conclusion, while challenges like the rising cost of labour may pose hurdles, the overall trajectory for industrial insulation in India is positive. As industries prioritize sustainability and energy efficiency, the demand for effective insulation solutions is likely to increase, providing ample opportunities for growth and innovation in the sector. The role of the insulation industry in India is set to be integral to the broader industrial landscape, contributing to a more sustainable and energy-efficient future.